P9-BJH-230

SACRED FOOTSTEPS

A TRAVELER'S GUIDE TO SPIRITUAL PLACES OF ITALY AND FRANCE

Melanie MacMitchell

OPAL STAR PRESS
Palo Alto ❖ Encinitas
California

Copyright © 1991 by Melanie MacMitchell.
All rights reserved. No part of this book may be reproduced or transmitted in any form or by any means, electronic or mechanical, including photocopying, recording, or by an information storage and retrieval system, without permission in writing from the publisher, except for the inclusion of brief quotations in a review.

Published by:
Opal Star Press
P.O. Box 231512
Encinitas, CA 92023-1512

Cover art: "Poppies," Tuscany, by Father Arthur Poulin, O.F.M.

Cover design by author and friends

Typography by Kathy Ryan

ISBN 0-9629727-0-3

Printed in the United States of America

For

My Song and My Protector

Acknowledgements

No writer has ever had a better friend than Marilee Rasmussen whose myriad gifts from cat feeding to correcting typos enabled this book to materialize. I am also so grateful to Leslie Hill for her in-depth editing and coaching; Jim McCavitt for his comments and valuable linkages to spiritual people and places; Arthur Poulin, O.F.M., for generously sharing his magnificent art; Ruth Donnelly for critically important suggestions; and Tom MacMitchell for loaning me his computer. Special thanks also to the many monastics and fellow pilgrims, too numerous to name, who cheered me on and whose enthusiasm for the spiritual life inspires my journey.

PREFACE

In the middle of the journey of our life I came to myself within a dark wood where the straight way was lost.
—Dante Alighieri, *The Divine Comedy*

At a midpoint in my life's path, I felt a deep need for greater inner peace. I was fortunate that after an intense decade of daily battles in a hostile management environment, I could pause to regain balance and pursue this goal.

To facilitate the change, I chose to go on a pilgrimage to spiritual places of Italy and France. I had previously travelled extensively as a tourist, and that kind of travel without a meaningful purpose now seemed an excessive investment of time, energy and money for little return. I had also been a pilgrim before to sacred places in the East and I had felt it bestowed refreshing expansion and joy.

There are places on the earth where great souls lived. Through long self-effort these souls attained exalted states of joy and love which truly are the divine birthright of each of us. Their lives have left a powerful imprint, like an eternal radiant sun, shining on these sites. Our own spiritual efforts are quickened and encouraged by walking in these souls' footsteps at their sacred sites.

"Pilgrimage" is a journey of love to spiritual places for the ultimate purpose of self-transformation. The journey is both an inner and outer one. Pilgrimage is a symbol of life: We are all seekers of the sacred, that which is holy, giving of wholeness or complete happiness, bliss. We travel on many diverse roads, yet knowingly or unknowingly share this common quest of the pilgrim.

There are over six thousand sanctuaries in Europe visited by over forty million people a year. For my pilgrimage to Italy and France, I chose to visit places which were mostly set in quiet locations of splendid natural beauty. In my pre-trip research about the sites, I could find no current guidebook which included affordable, harmonious lodging at or near each sanctuary. I know that many people who yearn to go on pilgrimage in Europe are discouraged by the high prices of travel there. Upon discovering and enjoying economical spiritual Retreat Houses, I wanted to share my findings so that others also might benefit.

So, Dear Readers, here is my offering. I hope that you will find it helps your search for greater inner and outer peace and that it furthers your journey, whether armchair or on-site, to the supreme sacred place: *"the Kingdom of God within."*

INTRODUCTION

One can't believe impossible things [said Alice]. I dare say you haven't had much practice, said the Queen. When I was your age, I always did it for half-an-hour a day. Why, sometimes I've believed as many as six impossible things before breakfast.
——Lewis Carroll, *Through the Looking Glass*

Each spiritual place in this book is introduced by brief stories of the life of the saint and/or supernatural event which occurred at the site. Many of these stories—apparitions, bilocations, levitations—seem impossible. It is not essential to believe the "impossible" in order to benefit from visiting sacred places. If you are sensitive and walk into a room where hideous violence has occurred you will feel it though you may not understand your feelings. Similarly, in places which radiate spiritual power, beneficial subtle forces inspire your consciousness to higher more noble states even though you may not be fully aware of this process.

At sacred sites you will see many outer signs of sanctity—crutches abandoned due to miraculous cures, evidence of stigmata, incorrupt bodies—which may seem bizarre. These certainly challenge our usual assumptions of reality and may encourage "belief in things unseen,*" or faith. Still, these outer phenomena are not the important part of the journey: The real miracle of pilgrimage occurs within the pilgrim. Unlike tourists grasping for outer momentos, pilgrims seek to open themselves in order to receive inner treasures. If we try to clear our minds of restless thoughts and our hearts of negative emotions through meditation and prayer at these sites, we enhance our receptivity to the renewing peace and joy all around us within and without.

*Hebrews 11:1

A summary of what to see at each sanctuary follows the brief historical description. Lodging at economical Retreat Houses is discussed in general in the next section of the book and a specific Retreat House is listed under each location.

Directions to the sanctuaries by car or public transport are also included for every chapter. Simplified maps of regions or towns accompany each section. These maps will guide you to the sanctuaries; however, especially if you are driving, an additional detailed road map is a good supplement. Michelin road maps, available in France and Italy, are excellent and are carried, or may be ordered, through most bookstores in the United States as well. For complete town maps go to the local tourist office listed in each chapter; usually they will supply you with a town map free of charge.

Every chapter concludes with notes on special holidays, festivals, musical events and other notable events at the sanctuaries.

It is my hope that the practicalities of your pilgrimage will be simplified by this guidebook and that your journey may include a new experience of the impossible.

I have learned this one lesson—that what is impossible with man is child's play with God and if we have faith in that Divinity...I have no doubt that all things are possible...

—Mahatma Gandhi

TABLE OF CONTENTS

TABLE OF CONTENTS (Cont'd.)

ILLUSTRATIONS

MAPS

GENERAL NOTES FOR THE PILGRIM:

SACRED SHELTER

After a day of exalting experiences, there is nothing worse than walking into a hotel where the raucous sounds and smells of the bar assail you and the manager tries to take advantage of your euphoria by price gouging.

Why not stay instead in a Spiritual Retreat House where the atmosphere of quiet and peace enables you to savor the day's meditative reflections?

The trade-off is that you will not have hotel amenities like radio, T.V., room service, or daily sheet changes. But you will have a clean, comfortable room, if not with a bath then with a spotless hot shower nearby, and at prices which will enable you to travel longer or return home underbudget.

Regardless of religious background, you can stay in Retreat Houses if you have reverence for holy sanctuaries, respect for various spiritual approaches, and a longing for inner peace.

Most Retreat Houses were once filled with monastic residents. Now, there may be only two or three monks or nuns living in an enormous facility. As a service and to make ends meet, the monasteries welcome pilgrims and often conduct seminars. Just as each monastic order varies, the Houses vary greatly in physical structure and ambiance. Some are modern dwellings; some are renovated buildings that have existed for centuries. In some, you can hear a pin drop; others are buzzing with an enthusiastic hush. You may find that your large window opens onto the snow-capped Pyrenees, a wild misty gorge in Auvergne, or ecstatic skylarks heralding the Umbrian dawn and dusk.

At every Retreat House, each room is usually furnished simply with a bed, nightstand and reading light, small desk, closet or armoire, and a sink. The greatest trial of your sacred shelter could be a very soft mattress—the benefits of firm ones are not yet widely established in Retreat Houses or for that matter, in small, economical hotels of France and Italy.

Due to inflation and currency fluctuations, the prices listed in the book must be taken only as guidelines. For Retreat Houses which list prices and for those that don't, however, you can count on paying considerably less than area hotels. Breakfast of coffee, bread, butter and jam is usually included in the nightly charge. Another meal, "demi-pension," or two other meals, "pension", is offered at some Retreats. Vegetarians may want to decline the usually nutritious meals unless they can arrange meat substitutes.

If you are travelling during the peak tourist seasons of summer, Christmas and Easter, it is best to reserve at least a month in advance at the Retreat Houses. Some people prefer pilgrimaging without a fixed schedule and are flexible enough to find other accommodations if they show up and the Retreat is full. While the Retreat Houses prefer advance reservations, they are usually understanding if a sincere pilgrim or two arrives unannounced.

It is recommended that you know a few pertinent phrases in French and Italian (those from a Berlitz language book will do). Little or no English is spoken at many Retreats. The limited English (or your French or Italian) which is known may be used initially to find out who you are, before accepting you. The monastics are truly receiving you into their home; they must feel comfortable that you will respect its hallowed purpose. Some monastics even give you a key; obviously, they must feel assured that House guests will consistently lock outside doors. The monastics intuitive scan, however, is usually done with such grace that it is barely noticeable.

The pilgrim is ordinarily welcome to join in as little or as much as he/she wants of certain aspects of the community life, such as Mass. One beauty of the Retreats is the respect accorded to solitude and privacy for everyone.

You could easily meet some of the most helpful, joyous people of your life in sacred shelters. And, lodging on these sacred grounds, you may realize further that ...

there is always a radiance in the soul of man, untroubled, like the light in a lantern in a wild turmoil of wind and tempest.

—Plotinus

GENERAL NOTES FOR THE PILGRIMS:

TRANSPORT TIPS

Travelling by car in Europe is less expensive than most people think if you lease, rather than rent, the car. For example, in 1991 to rent an economy car with manual transmission (Ford Fiesta, Peugeot 205, Citroen AX10 or VW Polo) from Budget-Rent-A-Car for more than 14 days for pickup in Paris, you will pay approximately $212 a week plus 22% French tax, plus $11 a day collision damage waiver, plus $5 a day passenger accident coverage and another $10 one time fee for each additional driver for an approximate total of $381 per week or $1143 for three weeks. You may prepay the base rate of $212 in U.S. dollars before you go abroad, and you must pay the taxes and insurance in France at whatever exchange rate prevails at the time of payment. You can only order car by category, for example, economy, and you must take what make of car is available when you pick it up.

By contrast, when you lease you choose the make of car and receive it brand new. For a 23 day lease of an economy car, manual transmission, the full cost would be $539. This price covers all tax, comprehensive public liability, fire and theft insurances, collision insurance with no deductible, personal and passenger insurances and emergency assistance according to Europe by Car, Inc. The paperwork for leasing is no more complicated than for rental. By the way, driving without insurance in Europe can get you into enormous difficulties if you have an accident, so be sure to carry it.

One drawback to car leasing is that the minimum lease period is 23 days. You can return the car before 23 days, however, and in doing so, your costs still might be less than car rental. With leasing, you must prepay in full six weeks before you pick up the car. Since the car is new, if you drive beyond a certain mileage you must have the oil and oil filter changed, a usual cost of $40-60; you are given a list of the numerous locations where your car can receive this service. Some of the lease companies listed at the end of this section give modest discounts for students, teachers and faculty and sometimes, you can obtain the prior year's lease rate if you pick up the car before April 1.

Although gas prices are considerably higher in Europe than the U.S. (during the Gulf War they rose to $4.75/gallon in France and $5.35/gallon in Italy), an economy car like a Citroen gets 47 miles per gallon. Also, distances between major cities in Europe are surprisingly close by comparison to major cities in the United States. For example, the distance between Rome and Geneva is similar to the distance between San Francisco and Los Angeles, about 400 miles.

There are road tolls for autoroutes in France and autostradas in Italy. Time permitting, the secondary roads in both these countries are an excellent alternative. They are usually toll-free, of good quality and more picturesque than the major highways.

If you do take the autostrade and autoroute, remember that the far left lane is strictly for passing. If you don't remember, a Porsche going 95 or 100 mph may bear down menacingly behind you before you know it. Also, avoid driving in major cities if you can. Driving outside them is no more difficult than driving in suburban America but even many French people do not dare drive in Paris (or Rome, Milan, etc.).

If you decide to travel by train be sure to look into the Eurailpass, the Eurail Saverpass and other special train fares. A basic general guidebook to France or Italy such as *Frommer's Dollarwise Guides* or the *Let's Go* series published by the Harvard Student Agencies Inc. can give you good initial information on train travel as well as on a variety of topics. Libraries usually carry these guidebooks. Most travel agents are well acquainted with Eurail passes.

The French and the Italian Government Tourist Offices in the U.S. also can be sources of a wide range of information. Ask them about special tours and events. A warning though—they are incredibly busy and their phone lines are too! You may want to write them instead of hearing the frustrating busy signal again and again. The French Government Tourist Office is located at 610 Fifth Ave., New York, NY 10020 (tel. 212-757-1125); 9454 Wilshire Blvd., Suite 303, Beverly Hills, CA 90212 (tel. 213-272-2661); 645 N. Michigan Ave., Chicago, IL 60601 (tel. 312-337-6301); and 2305 Cedar Spring Rd., Dallas, TX 75201 (tel. 214-720-4010). A recent note: If you call the French Tourist Office you will now get a recorded message which offers traveler information by calling 1-900-990-0040 at a charge of 50¢ per minute.

The Italian Government Travel Office is located at 630 Fifth Ave., New York, NY 10020 (tel. 212-245-4822); 360 Post St., San Francisco, CA 94108 (tel 415-392-6206) and 500 N. Michigan Ave., Chicago, IL 60611 (tel. 312-644-0990).

Car leasing agencies are:

Europe by Car, Inc. One Rockefeller Plaza, New York, NY 10020 (tel. 212-581-3040); Los Angeles (tel. 213-272-0424); San Francisco and San Diego (tel. 800-252-9401); Boston (tel. 800-637-9037); Washington, D.C., Seattle, Chicago (tel. 800-223-1516).

Auto Europe, Box 1097 Sharps Wharf, Camden, ME 04843 (tel. 800-223-5555; Canada 800-458-9503.

The Kemwel Group Inc., 106 Calvert St., Harrison, New York, NY 10528-3199 (tel. 800-678-0678; Canada (tel. 800-468-0468).

GENERAL NOTES FOR THE PILGRIM:

MONEY MATTERS

While every effort was made to ensure the accuracy of prices and travel information in this book, prices inflate, currencies fluctuate and information changes over time due to the many factors that affect travel.

There is no way to predict the exchange rates in France and Italy at the time you travel. Check with your bank, American Express or the Thomas Cook Foreign Exchange Office nearest to you to get the up-to-date rates. In June, 1991, the French unit of money, the franc (abbreviated F), was valued at 5.59F to $1 U.S. The Italian unit of money, the lira (abbreviated L), rate was L1200 to $1 U.S.

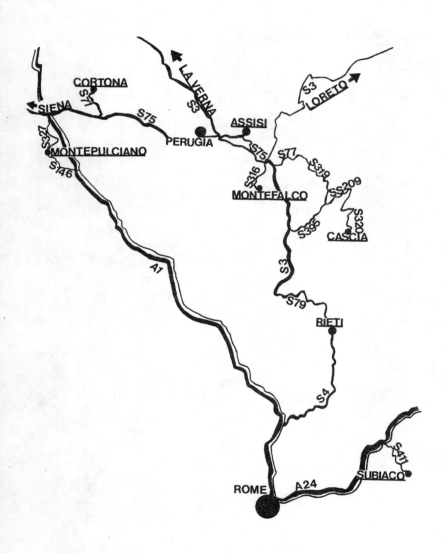

Sacred Sites in Umbria, Tuscany, Lazio

St. Francis of Assisi

I
ITALY

ASSISI

Sun and Moon -
Saint Francis and Saint Clare

Blessed be thou by God, o holy city, because many servants of God will dwell in thee and through thee many will be elected to the Kingdom of eternal life. Peace be with thee...
—St. Francis' blessing for Assisi

One day the people of Assisi saw a mass of light in the woods near their city. Thinking it was a forest fire, they rushed to put it out. As they neared the place of brilliance, they saw only the young Assisians Francis and Clare, surrounded by their followers, rapt in ecstasy; the intensity of their combined love for God cast an illuminating glow all around them. To the sensitive heart, the city of Assisi still shines with the radiant joy of St. Francis and St. Clare.

According to legend, in 1181 St. Francis' mother, Lady Pica, was in labor; yet, the baby would not be born. A pilgrim knocked on the door and said the child would arrive if Lady Pica went into the nearby stable. She did and Francis was born, like his Divine Master, in a cradle of straw.

Francis had a carefree youth with plenty of parties, friends and luxuries. His father was a wealthy merchant who wanted his son to become a businessman. A war began with the neighboring city of Perugia. With dreams of becoming a heroic knight, Francis went off to fight. He was captured and imprisoned for a year. After he returned to Assisi, he was persuaded again to go off to a war. However, in a dream he had in the town of Spoleto on the way to the battle, he was told to turn back to Assisi.

Sick and disillusioned, Francis returned to Assisi. He was twenty-four years old, still living at home, directionless. His former frivolities interested him no longer. He wandered through the beautiful hills of nearby Mount Subiaso, among wildflowers, high above lush valleys; still he could not find peace.

One day, praying before a crucifix in a dilapidated Church, the crucifix seemed to speak to him and say "Francis, go and repair my Church, which, as thou seest is a ruin. "[1]

Elated to receive a sign, a purpose, Francis rushed to his father's store. His father was away on one of his many buying trips so Francis took some bolts of expensive cloth and sold them in a nearby town. With this money, he planned to buy bricks and mortar to rebuild the Church of San Damiano where he had heard the crucifix speak to him.

Francis' father, Pietro Bernadone, was furious when he discovered his son's theft. He took Francis before the Bishop's Palace to demand restitution. A huge crowd watched as Francis returned his father's money and even the clothes Bernadone had given him. Francis, standing naked, declared that he now had only one father—a Heavenly Father.

Clare, the beautiful young daughter of an Assisi nobleman, was—like all of Assisi—aware of Francis' strange transformation. She watched for the next six years as Francis nursed lepers and rebuilt churches. Her own cousin Ruffino along with other Assisi youths had joined Francis' work. The Pope, inspired by a dream, had approved a brief religious Rule for the Brothers committed to poverty. Clare had managed to talk with Francis from time to time. He had told her "'You will have to know how to die...on the Cross of Christ.'"[2]

In 1212, nineteen year old Clare decided to join Francis' work. She chose to exit her noblehouse through a door called the Door of the Dead. Nearly all houses in Assisi had two doors — one for the living and one which was customarily closed. Only dead bodies passed feet first out of the house through the latter door. Symbolically, dying to her worldly life, Clare secretly left her home one night through the Door of the Dead and never returned.

Francis and the Brothers were waiting for Clare at the Porziuncola, one of their tiny rebuilt churches. Francis cut off Clare's long blond hair and traded her silken gown for a coarse one. Then he sent her to a nearby monastery. When her relatives learned of her flight, they stormed the monastery. Clare stood facing them, her right hand on the altar cloth, a sign of asylum in the Church. Her furious relatives threatened to take her by force until Clare took the black veil from her head, revealing that her beautiful hair was gone. Stunned and sorrowed by her commitment, the family retreated.

Francis soon sent Clare to San Damiano, which became the home of the Second Franciscan Order, the Poor Clares. Eventually, Clare was joined there by her younger sister, her mother and numerous other followers. Pledged to a love of poverty, she lived there for forty-two years.

Francis' followers now numbered thousands and many of them went on missionary trips throughout Europe. Francis went to Egypt and the Holy Land and met with the Moslem Sultan. When he returned to Italy in 1220, he had developed a severe eye disease. Francis had only six more years to live. According to one of his biographers, "He proposed to shun companionship with men and to retire to the most remote places, so that, having thus put off all cares and laid aside all solicitude for others, only the wall of flesh could stand between him and God."[3]

In one of these hermitages, La Verna, he received the stigmata, the sacred wounds of Christ.

In 1225, ailing, Francis returned to San Damiano to stay in a hut while Clare cared for him. Here he composed the Canticle of the Sun. However, his eyes worsened and painful medical cauterizations failed. Realizing he would die soon, Francis asked to be taken to the Porziuncola where, in 1226, he died.

As his body was being brought to Assisi, the Brothers stopped at San Damiano for Clare and the Sisters to kiss the stigmata wounds of his feet, his hands, his side. The spirit and love of St. Francis and St. Clare can still be felt in Assisi.

> *Lives of great men all remind us,*
> *we can make our lives sublime,*
> *And, departing, leave behind us*
> *footprints in the sands of time.*
> —Henry Wadsworth Longfellow,
> *A Psalm of Life*

St. Clare of Assisi

ASSISI

ASSISI
REGION: UMBRIA   PROVINCE: PERUGIA

The holy city located in the heart of Italy attracts numerous pilgrims and tourists year round. Its beautiful location, preserved medieval character and abundant pilgrim lodgings, make it an ideal base for visiting the many sacred sites nearby.

WHAT TO SEE

Basilica of St. Francis (San Francesco), Piazza San Francesco, 06081 Assisi. Open: Mornings and afternoons, daily.*

Work on the Basilica began two years after Francis' death when he was canonized; it was dedicated twenty-five years later in 1253.

The Lower Basilica gives access to the crypt where Francis is buried. The tombs of his followers Brothers Leo, Angelo, Masseo, Ruffino and Lady Jacoba are also in the crypt. During Francis' time, it was not uncommon for towns to steal the bodies of saints; his tomb was hidden until 1818.

The Upper Basilica contains the famous frescos by Giotto of the life of St. Francis.

The Rooms of St. Joseph of Copertino are located in the Sacro Convento (Sacred Convent) adjacent to the Basilica of St. Francis in Assisi.

St. Joseph, the seventeenth century saint of rapturous levitations witnessed by many, lived for seventeen years in the Franciscan monastery in Assisi. His preserved rooms are generally not open to the public. However, a devotee of the saint recently requested to see the rooms at the reception desk of the Basilica. When queried as to the purpose of the visit, the devotee replied, "I just love him," and a brief tour was promptly allowed.

Basilica of St. Clara (Santa Chiara), Piazza Santa Chiara, 06081 Assisi Open: Mornings and afternoons, daily.

* In Italy, "open mornings and afternoons" usually means from approximately 9am-1pm and approximately 4pm until 7pm.

Built on the site of a Church called San Giorgio where young Francis learned to read, the remains of St. Clare, discovered in 1850, are in the crypt. A small chapel to the right of the entrance contains relics of St. Clare and the crucifix that spoke to St. Francis in San Damiano.

Chiesa Nuova, Piazza Chiesa Nuova (just off the main Piazza del Commune). Open: Mornings and afternoons, daily.

The Church was built in 1615 to renovate the rooms where it is believed Francis lived until he was twenty-four. Facing the Church, a narrow lane to the left leads to the place thought to be the stable where Francis was born.

The Hermitage (L'Eremo delle Carceri) 2 miles from Assisi at 2,560 feet on the east side of Mt. Subasio. Open: Mornings and afternoons, daily.

The road to the Hermitage leaves Assisi at Porta dei Capuccini; it rises gradually through olive groves, cypresses, oak and broom to reach a little monastery and series of caves tucked in the woods. St. Francis frequently came here for solitude; the grotto where he slept on a rock can be visited as well as the caves where the other Brothers dwelt.

Monastery of San Damiano (Convento di S. Damiano), 1 mile outside of Assisi through the Porta Nuova; follow signs. Open: Mornings and afternoons, daily.

San Damiano, still a working convent, is essentially unchanged from the days of St. Clare and St. Francis. The Church, the refectory, the garden and the Sisters' dormitory, where a wooden cross and flowers mark the place St. Clare died, are all open to the public.

St. Mary of the Angels (Santa Maria degli Angeli), 3 miles south of Assisi to the southwest; follow signs. Open: Mornings and afternoons, daily.

The Basilica was built in the sixteenth century around the *Porziuncola*, the tiny chapel restored by Francis' own hands. In the *Chapel of the Transitus*, now inside the Basilica, Francis died. Follow a corridor to the right of the

Chapel past a statue of St. Francis in which white doves nest. This path goes past the rose bushes which became thornless after Francis threw himself into them to resist temptation. At the end of the path is the *Chapel of the Rosebushes*. It was built by St. Bonaventure, a follower of St. Francis, around the site of a hut where St. Francis frequently prayed.

HOW TO GET THERE

By car: Assisi is approximately 105 miles from Rome (2 1/2 hours) 285 miles from Milan (4 hours). Cars can be rented at the Rome or Milan airports (or in Perugia or Florence). If ever there is a reason to rent a car during your travels it is to see the beautiful Umbrian and Tuscan countryside while visiting the numerous sacred sites in this area. From Rome to Assisi take Autostrade A1 to route S75 or, try the backroads and stop at S4, S79, and S3 to S75 and stop at the Rieti Valley sanctuaries described in the next chapter.

By public transport: Train, get off at Station Santa Maria degli Angeli, 3 miles from Assisi. Railway connections from Rome and Florence are likely to involve changing trains at Foligno (Assisi is on the Foligno-Terontola line). Buses go to Assisi every 1/2 hour from the train station to Assisi. Taxis: (tel. 804-0275) are also available. Buses travel to Assisi from Rome, Florence, Siena, Perugia, Spello, Foligno, etc. If you don't like changing trains, you may find travelling by bus preferable in Italy.

WHERE TO STAY

St. Antony's Guest House (Franciscan Sisters of the Atonement), Via Galeazzo Alessi n. 10, 06081 Assisi (tel. 075-812-542).

English speaking, toilet and shower usually within the room, English library, chapel, gardens, parking off-site within walking distance, elevator. L32,000 per person including breakfast of coffee and rolls. Central location near the Piazza del Commune. Ask for a room with view of the Basilica of Saint Clare; hundreds of skylarks love to circle its rose colored stones at dawn and dusk.

Monastery of Saint Colette (Monastero S. Colletta), Borgo S. Pietro 3, 06081 Assisi (tel. 075-812-345

French speaking primarily, although some English is spoken. Large facilities and gardens, views. Chapel, primarily French library. Central location near Piazza San Pietro. L20,000 per person for a single room including breakfast, with bath and shower separate. Some rooms have incredible views overlooking the Umbrian countryside.

Casa Papa Giovanni (House of Pope John), Via S. Paolo 32, 06081 Assisi (tel. 075-812-467).

Italian speaking primarily, some English. Modern building with elevator, meditation garden, bookstore on site, chapel, parking off-site within walking distance. Central location near the Piazza del Commune. L20,000 per person, breakfast included; separate shower and bath. Pension and demi-pension also available.

Reservations are recommended for the Assisi Retreat Houses, especially during summer and holidays. During winter, November through February, the houses may close for part of the time. Contact the Retreat House directly for availability.

The Other Assisi

A smiling Tibetan Buddhist monk in ochre garb and a gentle-faced Pope in white robes tenderly embrace in a photograph that hangs in the reception room of the Basilica of St. Francis in Assisi. The picture was taken in the early 1970's when Pope John Paul II assembled an international religious conference on world peace in Assisi. This conference augmented Assisi's role as a holy place nurturing diverse approaches to inner and outer peace.

Unsurprisingly, in the shelter of sacred Mt. Subiaso, an "other Assisi" lives. Scattered around the mountain are communities of Tibetan Buddhists, yogis, Catholics living in silence, and ecumenical lay people modeling their lives after the early Franciscan friars. Some of these communities prefer to live semi-hidden while other groups accept pilgrims for spiritual retreats. Two such communities are listed here; an adventure awaits the pilgrim seeking to discover the many faces of the "other Assisi. "

The Community of Carlos Caretto (Piccoli Fraternità San Girolano), 06038 Spello (tel. 0742-652-719). Call for directions to the Community.

Carlos Caretto was a leader in Italian Catholic organizations. At age forty-four he felt called to the African desert to join the Brothers of Jesus founded by Charles de Foucauld. Eventually, he returned to Europe to help the multitudes of youth seeking meaning during the 1960's. On the southern slopes of Mt. Subiaso near Spello, he started a small community patterned after the early Brothers of St. Francis. Silence and sharing, prayer and work are the focus of daily life.

Though Carlos Carretto is no longer living, his community is thriving. Increasing numbers of Europeans join them for week-long retreats held throughout the year.

Fratellanza Della Gioia (Fraternity of Joy), Casella Postale 48, 06088 Santa Maria degli Angeli (tel. 9742-811-212).

This community of Americans and Europeans, called Ananda in The United States, welcomes retreatants interested in the path of Raja Yoga. It is located in a beautiful setting in San Presto, 11 miles from Assisi (about a half hour drive). If driving, follow direction to Gualdo Tadino on road 444. The main building is well marked near the road. By public transport: Bus from Assisi. Each weekday at 1:55pm a bus leaves from Piazza Matteotti. Get off at Montemezzo in front of Il Rifugio sign which is in front of the Fratellanza.

Photo in the reception room of the bascilica of St. Francis, Assisi

Oh, East is East, and West is West, and never the twain shall meet... But there is neither East nor West, Border nor Breed, nor Birth when two strong men stand face to face, tho they come from the ends of the earth.

—Rudyard Kipling

TOURIST OFFICE

Azienda di Promozione Turistica di Assisi, Piazza del Commune 12, 06081 Assisi (tel. 075-812-534). Open: Mornings and afternoons, daily.

NOTES

October 4 is the Feast Day** of St. Francis, Patron Saint of Ecology; August 11 is the Feast Day of St. Clare. Every June 22 there is a procession to the monastery of San Damiano to commemorate the routing of the Saracens by St. Clare.

For three days beginning with the first Tuesday, Assisi celebrates Calendimaggio. The festival is a colorful evocation of medieval games, costumes, dances, processions, serenades and flag display. During the last two weeks of July and the first week in August, Assisi hosts vocal and instrumental concerts and musical courses and seminars. Reservations for lodging during these periods of time, and during Easter week, must be made well in advance.

** A saint's Feast Day is usually an occasion of pilgrim processions, special celebrations and services at the saint's sanctuary. It can be celebrated on the Feast Day or on the Sunday closest to the Feast Day. This local religious holiday usually doesn't close shops and businesses, but it can make accommodations crowded. On national holidays (and Sundays) most shops and businesses do close in Italy; restaurants do not close. These holidays are: January 1; January 6 (Epiphany); Easter Monday; April 25 (Liberation Day); May 1 (Labor Day); August 15 (Ferragosto—Assumption of the Blessed Virgin Mary); November 1 (All Saints Day); December 8 (Immaculate Conception of the Blessed Virgin Mary); December 25 and 26.

II

ITALY

RIETI VALLEY

Franciscan Hermitages

REGION: LAZIO   **PROVINCE: RIETI**

The traveler may want to further explore the life of St. Francis in the lovely Rieti Valley, a day trip from Assisi or Rome. Caves and hermitages where St. Francis sought solitude are secluded in four mountain slopes surrounding the Rieti Valley. Simplicity and serenity still characterize the holy valley sixty-eight miles southeast of Assisi and forty-eight miles from Rome. From Assisi, take S75 to Foligno and S3 by Spoleto to Terni; then follow directions listed below for each sanctuary.

The Sanctuary of Poggio Bustone (Convento di Poggio Bustone). Open: Mornings and afternoons, daily. Located six miles north of Rieti by the Terni road. At Terni, follow signs to Rieti. After about seven miles there will be signs and a road to the left to Poggio Bustone. Continue through the village of Poggio Bustone up the winding road. The monastery is located at 2,684 feet, in a lovely setting.

Francis and his companions first arrived here in the summer of 1208. *The Grotto of the Revelations* or *Upper Sanctuary* is about a half hour walk from the little square in front of the monastery. Here, Francis learned that his sins were pardoned by God and that his order of Friars Minor would expand. From Poggio Bustone he sent forth the first band of men announcing peace.

The Original Hermitage or *Inferior Sanctuary* is a thirteenth century convent. To the right of the main cloister entrance are stairs descending to caves used by the first disciples of St. Francis.

The Sanctuary of S. Maria de La Foresta (Convento La Foresta). Open: Mornings and afternoons, daily. From Rieti, follow the signs to La Foresta which is three miles north.

A miracle occurred at La Foresta: In the summer of 1225, St. Francis was on his way to Fonte Columbo to have his eyes cauterized. Approaching Rieti, he learned that a crowd of people were gathering to see him; reluctant, he slipped away for seclusion to La Foresta. There, a priest agreed to take him in. However, the crowds pursued Francis and trampled the priest's vineyards. Francis saw that the priest regretted accepting him and so Francis asked him how many loads of grapes he had expected from the harvest. When the priest replied twelve, Francis promised that he would now receive twenty loads. Despite decimated vines, at grape-gathering time, twenty loads of the best grapes were collected by the priest.

A little cave used by Francis and a Domus (Hospital House) used by Francis and his companions can be visited at La Foresta.

The Sanctuary of Fonte Colombo (Convento di Fonte Colombo). Open: Mornings and afternoons, daily. Three miles to the southwest of Rieti is Fonte Colombo or Fountain of Doves. Take the road toward Contigliano and after about two miles turn left. Follow signs to the sanctuary.

Francis came to this site for an unsuccessful attempt to stop the loss of his eyesight. Just before the cauterization with a hot branding iron, Francis prayed to Brother Fire for protection. Although his companions fled upon witnessing the gruesome operation, Francis afterwards said he had not felt any pain or heat.

In the sacred cave here, Francis wrote his third Rule for the Franciscan Order and received confirmation of it by an appearance of Lord Jesus. Thus, Fonte Colombo is called the "Franciscan Sinai" because, like Moses receiving the tablets of law from God, Francis received the law for his followers.

The Sanctuary of Greccio. Open: Mornings and afternoons, daily. Nine miles northwest of Rieti on the Contigliano road toward Terni. About one mile from the town of Contigliano is the village of Greccio. The Franciscan Sanctuary of Greccio is located about one mile from the village. Park at the esplanade at the foot of the monastery.

This sanctuary is considered sacred because, on Christmas Eve, 1223, Francis, the brothers and villagers celebrated Christ's birth with live animals in a cave there. The infant Jesus appeared in Francis' arms to some of those present. The *Crib Chapel* is built on the site of this vision. The original convent where Francis and his companions lived also is preserved.

WHERE TO STAY

Rieti Valley is a lovely daytrip from Assisi. However, there is also a retreat house on a hill about one mile from Rieti if you wish to stay overnight in the area.

The Oasis of St. Antony on the Mountain, Casa di Esercizi "St. Antonio", S. Antonio al Monte, 02100 Rieti (tel. 0746-43-238). Take a bus or train to Rieti and taxi to this retreat house.

NOTES

Every Saturday from mid-June to mid-September, there is an excursion bus from Assisi to Greccio, Fonte Columbo and La Foresta. The bus leaves Assisi at approximately 8am and returns at 8pm; cost is about L27,000. Inquire at the Tourist Office in Assisi for further information.

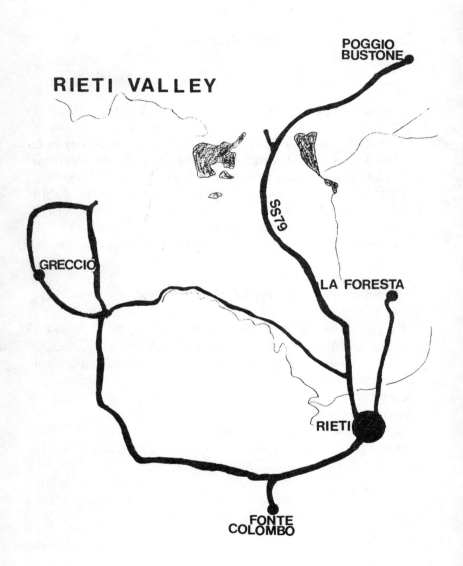

RIETI VALLEY

POGGIO
BUSTONE

SS79

GRECCIO

LA FORESTA

RIETI

FONTE
COLOMBO

III
ITALY

LA VERNA

The Sigmata of St. Francis of Assisi

REGION: TUSCANY   **PROVINCE: AREZZO**

Also possible to visit as a daytrip from Assisi is La Verna. La Verna, one of St. Francis' favorite mountain hermitages is where he received the stigmata of Lord Jesus in 1224. It includes a Basilica with many Della Robbia terracottas, the Chapel of the Stigmata, the cave where St. Francis slept and his first cell where Christ appeared, and other sacred sites set amid majestic woods of beech and pine.

HOW TO GET THERE

By car: Route S3, exit Pieve S. Stefano, approximately 43 miles from Assisi (follow S3 in the direction of Cesena when travelling from Assisi). La Verna is 53 miles from Florence; 165 miles from Rome. At Pieve S. Stefano, follow signs to La Verna, about 13 miles along a winding picturesque road.

By public transport: Every Tuesday from mid-June through mid-September, there is an excursion bus from Assisi to La Verna. The cost is approximately L32,000. Inquire at the Assisi Tourist Office for further details. Otherwise, it is difficult to reach La Verna by public transport.

WHERE TO STAY

Refettoria del Pellegrino (Santuario della Verna), 52010 Chiusi della Verna (tel. 0575-599-356). A large pilgrim's house open all year. If the information center is closed, inquire at the coffee bar for accommodations. Single room with bath is about L23,000. Pension and demi-pension available.

Courtyard at La Verna

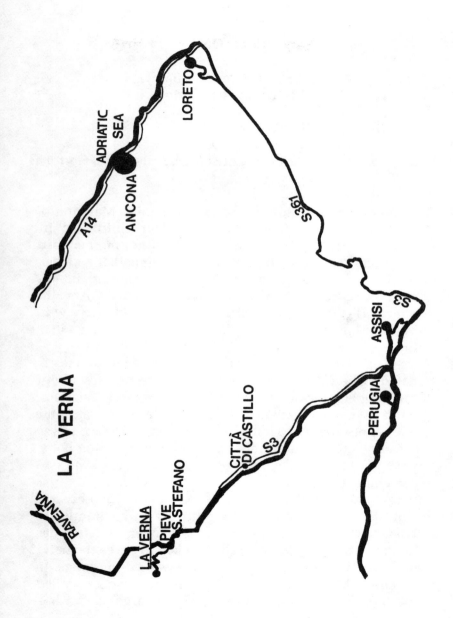

IV
ITALY

CORTONA

A Sinner Becomes a Saint -
St. Margaret of Cortona

*Thou art the third light granted to
the order of my beloved Francis.*
   —Vision of Christ to St. Margaret of Cortona

In an unusual early life for a future saint, Margaret of
Cortona bore an illegitimate son. Her childhood in
Laviano, Tuscany had been happy until her mother died
when she was eight. Then, an abusive stepmother and lack
of affection created great suffering for the beautiful, intelli-
gent Margaret. A handsome nobleman named Arsenio
appeared when she was sixteen and she ran off to live with
him in Montepulciano. A year later, she bore their son at
the age of seventeen.

Apparently, Arsenio promised marriage but procrasti-
nated. The finely dressed Margaret rode proudly about
town, openly acknowledging that she was his mistress.
After nine years together, Arsenio failed to return home
one night. Margaret followed their dog to a place in the
forest where eventually she found Arsenio's rotting body,
partially buried. For reasons never discovered, he had
been murdered.

Arsenio's relatives soon banished Margaret and her son
from their noblehouse. She returned to her family in
Laviano but they also rejected her. An inner voice told her
to go to Cortona. By now, she had begun to see the hand
of God in her circumstances and she wanted to change. In
Cortona, she met a group of compassionate women called
the Moscari Sisterhood. They took in Margaret and her

son, and turned her spiritual care over to the Franciscan Friars Minor in Cortona.

With their help, Margaret began radical inner transformation. She made her living by caring for the sick. After three years of a devout life, she was accepted into the order of lay Franciscans. Her son went to school in nearby Arezzo and later became a monk.

Eventually the example of Margaret's life became a "brilliant light" for the Third Franciscan Order. She founded a hospital and those who had previously scorned her now sought her sage counsel. In a vision, she learned she was to spend the rest of her life in seclusion in an abandoned oratory on a hill above Cortona. For nine years she lived there experiencing ecstatic states, dialogues with Christ, and being the instrument of miraculous cures. She died in 1297 at age fifty. Almost seven hundred years after her death, her incorrupt body rests in the Basilica dedicated to her on a hill above Cortona.

Besides St. Margaret, St. Francis also played a role in Cortona's history. He had a monastery built two miles from Cortona and he stayed there several times, as did his followers St. Bonaventure, St. Antony of Padua and the Blessed Guido. In 1226, St. Francis stayed in this hermitage on his final journey from Siena to Assisi.

The Church of St. Francis in Cortona contains a large wood piece purported to be from the actual Cross of Christ, as well as the first representation of St. Margaret in fresco.

Self conquest is the greatest of victories.

—Plato

St. Margaret of Cortona

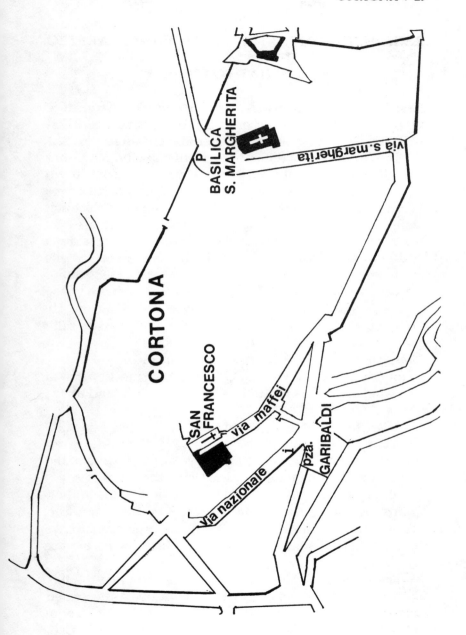

CORTONA
REGION: TUSCANY   **PROVINCE: AREZZO**

WHAT TO SEE

Basilica of Saint Margaret of Cortona (Santuario di S. Margherita), Via S. Margherita, 52044 Cortona (tel. 0575-603-116). Open: Mornings and afternoons, daily.

The Sanctuary is outside the medieval city just under the ruins of the old fort, a steep walk from town (approximately 20 minutes) past stations of the cross. Driving, follow the road that runs alongside the old town walls and the signs to the Sanctuary or Basilica of St. Margherita. A panoramic view of Tuscan countryside is visible from the Sanctuary. The Basilica is built on the site of the oratory where the Saint spent the last nine years of her life in seclusion. Though discolored, her corpse remains intact (including whole eyes and nails) nearly seven hundred years after her death; it is in a glass reliquary, a receptacle, under the main altar.

Church of St. Francis (Chiesa di San Francesco).

Within the medieval walls of Cortona at the junction of Via G. Maffei and Via Berrettini. Open: Mornings and afternoons, daily.

The Church was begun in 1245 by Brother Elias, St. Francis' companion, and was frequented by St. Margaret. A centuries old fresco by an unknown artist of her is at the rear of the Church on the left side facing the doors.

A large piece of the Holy Cross is in this Italian Church. It was carried from Jerusalem by the Franciscan Brother Elias. The relic is kept in an ornamental case behind the main altar and is only open for viewing on rare occasions.

There are also relics of St. Francis (a habit and the pillow given to him by his follower Lady Jacopa as he neared death) in a room to the left of the main altar. In a room behind the main altar, Brother Elias' bones are buried under a stone in the floor; these rooms can be visited with the permission of the monk usually on the premises.

Franciscan Cell Hermitage (Eremo Francescano delle Celle). Open: Mornings and afternoons, daily.

Francis stayed here on his last journey from Siena to Assisi. His tiny cell is preserved. The Hermitage is located approximately two miles from Cortona. Follow the road outside the town wall that leads to the Sanctuary of St. Margaret. Watch carefully for a poorly paved dirt road to the left just as there is a sharp right turn in the road and it begins to climb toward the Sanctuary. There may be a faded yellow sign on the left with the word "Celle" barely visible. Follow the narrow poorly paved road until you reach the hermitage gates on the right. Park outside the gates. The hermitage is a typical Franciscan retreat built into rock, isolated in woods and located alongside a river. Today, the monastery is occupied by the Capuchin Order of Franciscans.

HOW TO GET THERE

By car: Cortona is just off road S71 not far from Autostrade A1 which runs between Florence and Rome. From Assisi, Cortona is easily reached by taking S75 past Perugia to S71 (approximately 45 miles, one hour).

By public transport: Train, Station Terontola-Cortona (about 6 miles south of Cortona). Fast Rome-Florence trains stop here. Shuttle buses go to Piazza Garibaldi in Cortona. On local trains, arrive at Station Camucia-Cortona, approximately 4 miles from town and bus to Cortona from the station.

WHERE TO STAY

Cortona is a lovely daytrip through Tuscan and Umbrian countryside from Assisi. Or check out:
Oasi Giovanni Neumann, Via Contesse 1, 52044 Cortona (tel. 0575-63-118).

TOURIST OFFICE

AAST, Via Nazionale 72 (off Piazza Garibaldi). Open: Mon.-Sat., 8:30am-12:30pm and 3-6pm.

NOTES

February 22 is the Feast Day of St. Margaret. Cortona is a well preserved medieval Tuscan hilltown. The area around St. Margaret's sanctuary near the summit of the town overlooks terraces of vines and olives; it is a lovely location for a picnic.

V

ITALY

CASCIA

Pilgrimages to the Perfume Saint - St. Rita

The most powerful form of energy one can generate is prayer. Prayer, like radium, is a luminous and self generating form of energy.
— Dr. Alexis Carrell, Nobel prize winner in Medicine

The Saint of the Impossible, St. Rita, draws busloads of pilgrims to Cascia on her Feast Day each May. Devotees walk in candlelight processions, dance, celebrate and offer roses and prayers before the incorrupt body of the "perfume" saint.

Shortly after Rita was born near Cascia in 1386, bees swarmed in and out of her cradle without harming her. As she grew in childhood, she preferred pilgrimages to holy places rather than children's games. She wanted to be a nun but her elderly parents elected marriage for her at age twelve, to a man who turned out to be abusive and unfaithful. Rita bore two sons and endured the marriage twenty-two years until her husband was assassinated. Her sons vowed the customary Italian vendetta. Rita, failing to dissuade them from becoming murderers, prayed that their lives be taken first. Her sons soon became ill, forgave their enemies and died.

Shortly after their deaths, Rita went to the Augustinian convent in Cascia and asked to be accepted as a nun. The Sisters didn't admit widows and Rita was rejected. She prayed for the impossible and one night she was visited by her three favorite saints. John the Baptist accompanied by Saints Augustine and Nicholas of Tolentino, led her in the night to the locked convent and miraculously opened its doors for her. The astonished Sisters found Rita there in the morning and decided that her unprecedented entry was God's proof of her place with them.

Rita spent the rest of her life as an Augustinian nun. In 1443, she wounded her forehead on a thorn which was part of a statue of Christ. The wound also is explained supernaturally as a stigmata. Regardless of origin, it became odorous, ugly and never healed. It was so offensive that Rita had to live fifteen years of her life in near seclusion. She performed her convent duties, prayers and worship in solitude, using her isolation to deepen her relationship with God.

A lingering final illness, probably cancer, also was borne by Rita with equanimity. Shortly before her death at age seventy-six, in the frigid depths of winter, beautiful roses bloomed in her little monastery garden. At the moment of her death, an astounding light emanated from the wound in her forehead. After her passing, her body exuded a fragrant sweet odor and has remained incorrupt for over 350 years. Many miracles have been experienced by devotees as the result of her powerful intervention.

And all things, whatsoever ye shall ask in prayer, believing, ye shall receive.

—Matthew 21:22

St. Rita's Rock, Roccaporena

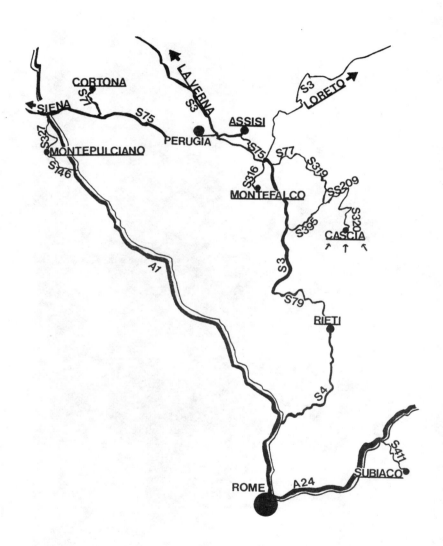

CASCIA
REGION: UMBRIA   PROVINCE: PERUGIA

WHAT TO SEE

The Basilica of St. Rita (Santuario di Santa Rita). Open: Mornings and afternoons daily.

In the Basilica, built in 1946, to the left of the altar, lies St. Rita's incorrupt body.

St. Rita's Monastery (Il Monastero di S. Rita), adjacent to the Basilica, is still occupied by Augustinian nuns. Open: Mornings and afternoons, daily. St. Rita's cell and various other relics can be visited in the monastery.

In the hamlet of *Roccaporena*, three miles from Cascia, is the *House of St. Rita* (Casa di S. Rita) where the saint was born; it is now a tiny chapel.

St. Rita's Rock (Lo Scoglio di S. Rita) on a high crag above Roccaporena is enclosed within a small chapel. Apparently, Rita often made the steep, approximately 1/2 hour climb, to this rock to pray. There is also a grotto in Roccaporena which Rita used to frequent. It is visible from the road, marked with a large cross.

HOW TO GET THERE

By car: From Assisi (approximately 66 miles, 2 hours) take road S75 to Foligno. At Foligno, follow the signs in the direction of Macerata (S77). Signs indicating Cascia soon begin to appear. Follow road S319 to SS209 and S320 into town; once in town, the way to the Basilica is well marked. Cascia is 87 miles from Rome.

By public transport: From mid-June to mid-September, an excursion bus leaves from Assisi once a week for a day visit to Spoleto, Norcia, Casica, and Roccaporena. Inquire at the tourist office in Assisi; purchase tickets in advance. Otherwise, Cascia is difficult to reach by public transport. Train, get off at Station Spoleto (approximately 30 miles from Assisi) and then transfer to bus. There are six buses daily to Norcia (the birthplace of St. Scholastica and St. Benedict) which is about 11 miles from Cascia; some of the buses have connections to Cascia. From Cascia there are local buses to Roccaporena. Buses also travel from Rome to Cascia. Inquire at Contram Camerino, Via Palestro 5, Rome (tel. 0644-51-800).

WHERE TO STAY

Casa del Pellegrino (Pilgrim's House), Via Santuario S. Rita 90, 06043 Roccaporena (tel. 0743-71-205). 85 rooms, 148 beds, restaurant, garden, parking, elevator. 3 miles from Cascia. L37,000-40,000 for a single room with private bath or shower; L53,000-56000 for double room with private bath or shower. Pension and demi-pension available.

TOURIST OFFICE

Azienda di Promozione Turistica Valnerina, Via Vespasia Polla, 06043 Cascia (near Piazza Garibaldi) (tel. 0743-71-147).

NOTES

Cascia is a village of four thousand people where men still play folk melodies on accordions outside shops to the clapping admiration of their friends. On May 22, the Feast Day of St. Rita, thousands of small oil lamps are lit on buildings all over Cascia during a candlelight procession to Roccaporena; there are many other festivities as well during this time.

VI
ITALY

SIENA

Doctor of the Church -
St. Catherine

*In all your works put God before your eyes saying... [the body]
must die, and knowest not when; and [must] render account
before the highest Judge...who punishes every fault and rewards
every good deed.*

—St. Catherine of Siena, *Letters*

Catherine, the twenty-third child of a Sienese dyer,
lived only thirty-three years. Yet in that brief span the
uneducated woman counselled Popes and royalty, nego-
tiated peace between warring cities and wrote works of
such importance that in 1970 she was honored posthu-
mously as one of two women Doctors of the Roman
Catholic Church.

St. Catherine of Siena's astonishing public activities are
only surpassed by her exalted inner achievements. Her
mystical experiences began in 1353 at age six, when she
saw Christ and the Saints Peter, Paul and John above the
Church of St. Dominic in Siena.

At age 18, the attractive Catherine became a member of
the Dominican lay order. Miracles, levitations, ecstatic raptures were a normal part of her extraordinary life. She
served by caring for prisoners and the sick as well, and
during the plague of 1372 she nursed and buried victims
with her own hands.

When Catherine travelled, three confessors accompanied her because so many people were spontaneously
converted in her presence. She received the stigmata during her lifetime though these holy wounds of Christ were
visible only to Catherine until her death. After her death in

Rome in 1380, the fresh wounds on her hands, feet and side appeared clearly to all who saw her body. The stigmata were visible proof of Catherine's belief that every good deed would be rewarded: Her life of attunement with Christ was rewarded by these rare visible signs of holiness. Five centuries after her death, the essayist Emerson reiterated this principle of "reaping what you sow."

The world looks like...a mathematical equation... Every secret is told, every crime punished, every virtue rewarded, every wrong redressed in silence and certainty.
—Ralph Waldo Emerson, *Compensation*

House of St. Catherine of Siena (at end of street)

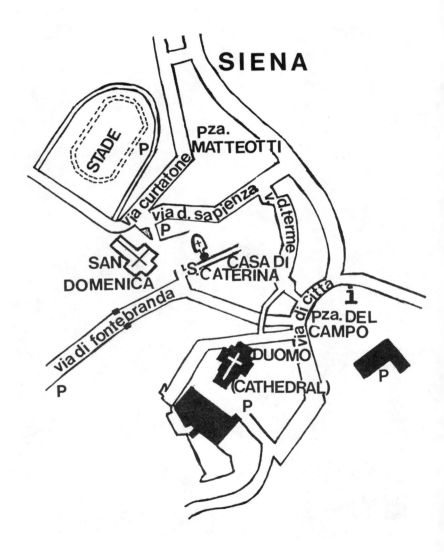

SIENA
REGION: TUSCANY   PROVINCE: SIENA

WHAT TO SEE

The House of St. Catherine of Siena (La Casa di Santa Caterina). Via di Santa Caterina (near San Domenico's Basilica). Open: Mornings and afternoons throughout the year, donation.

"Sponsae Christi, Katherinae Domus" ("this is the house of Catherine bride of Christ") is inscribed over the door at the house where St. Catherine lived. Beneath the interior stairs is the cell where she lived in seclusion for three years. Other relics of the saint, such as a walking stick and lantern she used when travelling in the city to visit the sick, are in the house. *Basilica of St. Dominic* (San Domenico) Open: Mornings and afternoons, daily.

Above this Church, Catherine saw her first vision. Her head is in a chapel in the Basilica, halfway down the south aisle. She had many trances in San Domenico's Bascilica.

HOW TO GET THERE

By car: Easily reachable from several major roads. Follow signs to Stade (stadium). San Domenico and St. Catherine's house are near the stadium in the southwest area of Siena. There is parking also in the area. Cars are restricted from driving through the center of Siena, a preserved medieval city.

By public transport: Train, Station Siena (about 1½ miles from the city center), lines Florence/Pisa. Buses from the station shuttle to Place Matteotti which is within walking distance of San Domenico. Buses from out of town arrive and leave from a station by San Domenico (buy tickets in advance).

WHERE TO STAY

Daytrip from Assisi (approximately 70 miles) or try:
Villa Santa Regina Strada Viglano 6, (tel. 0577-22-12-06).
A pilgrim's house, often full. Siena is a major tourist stop
and if accommodations are booked try the Cooperativa
"Hotels Promotion" booth opposite the Bascilica of San
Domenico (tel. 0577-28-80-84) which provides a list of
rooms in private homes.

TOURIST OFFICE

AAST, Via di Citta 43 (tel. 0577-28-05-51). Located near the
heart of medieval Siena, the Piazza del Campo. Open:
Mornings and afternoons, daily.

NOTES

April 29 is the Feast Day of St. Catherine of Siena. On
July 2 and August 16, Siena holds its famous Palio, a bare-
back horse race lasting less than a minute yet preceded by
days of sometimes brutal preparatory rites, races and
medieval pageantry. The festival is primarily for residents
not tourists. Most spectators must wait long hours crushed
in crowds along the racetrack rails for a view of the race.
Accommodations in Siena are difficult to find during the
weeks surrounding these events.

VII
ITALY

MONTEFALCO

Visionary of the Cross -
St. Clare

*If you seek the cross of Christ, take my heart;
there you will find the suffering Lord.*
—St. Clare of the Cross

In the midst of woods, olive trees and vines, Montefalco, like its name, mount of falcons, perches over tranquil Umbrian countryside. In 1271, a twenty year old woman named Giovanna Vengente and her friend Andreola went to live as contemplatives in a hermitage near Montefalco. Soon, Giovanna's six year old sister, Clare, joined them.

The community of holy women grew and a larger hermitage was acquired in the town. Several other religious communities in Montefalco, fearing competition for alms, slandered Giovanna's little group. As a result, the community was forced to beg in the countryside and subsist for a while on scant herbs and grains. Beautiful Clare, now fifteen, volunteered to beg, though the countryside was known as a place where violence befell defenseless people. For forty days, Clare begged unharmed until her sister forbade her to risk her life any longer; Clare never again left the cloister.

At age twenty, Clare was plunged into a long period of spiritual darkness and discouragement. This state continued for over a decade. Her parents and sister died during this time and Clare, against her wishes, was elected abbess of the community. In 1290, the recluses were forced by the Church hierarchy to choose an approved rule; they adopted the Rule of St. Augustine which "is characterized by a common life lived in a unity of mind and heart fixed on God."4

Though her communication with the outside world was always from behind a grille, Clare's wisdom began to be known throughout the region. People of every social level sought her counsel. She never showed any liking for this esteem nor displeasure at the inevitable persecution and calumny that also were directed at her community on occasion.

In 1294, she suddenly entered a deep mystical state lasting several weeks. Her sisters had to feed her sugared water to keep her alive during this period. In this ecstasy, Christ appeared to her and told her "I have searched the world for a strong place to plant firmly this cross...Yes, Clare, I have found a place for my cross."5

In the last years of her life, Clare's intense suffering became great joy. Though she was physically ill much of the time, she would often break forth in joyous song. On the day of her death she was well, talking with a Franciscan monk. *"'Now I have nothing more to say to you...I am going to Him."'*6 With these words, Clare turned her eyes upward and left her body without a quiver. When her heart was removed, the cardiac tissue was distinctly composed in the form of a Cross.

"The life of the soul is the love of God"
—St. Clare of the Cross

St. Clare of the Cross, Montefalco

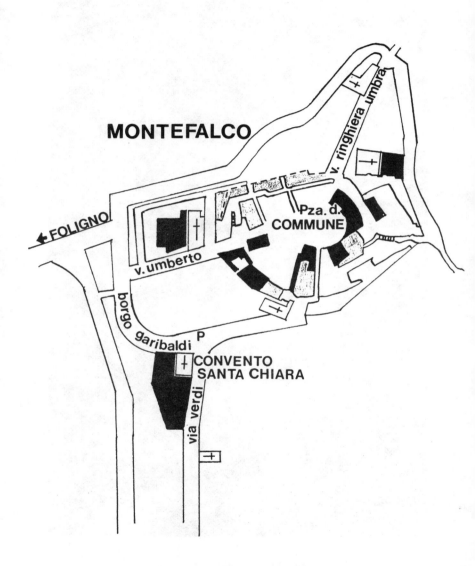

MONTEFALCO

REGION: UMBRIA   PROVINCE: PERUGIA

WHAT TO SEE

Church of the Holy Cross (Church of St. Clare, Santa Chiara), Convento di Santa Chiara, 06036 Montefalco (tel. 0742-790-123). Open: Mornings and afternoons, daily.

The incorrupt body and heart of St. Clare of the Cross rest in this Church. If there is no Sister present in the bookroom to the right of the main entrance, ring the bell on the left side of the bookroom wall. If the Sisters are not in prayers, they will come and show you the relics of St. Clare. Also, they may show you the *Chapel of the Holy Cross* (St. Croce Chapel) where St. Clare died (through a door to the left side of the main altar) and the cloister. Within the cloister, there is a tree, apparently of Himalayan origin, which is the only one of its kind growing wild in Europe; its berries are used by the nuns to make rosaries and are purported to have healing qualities.

HOW TO GET THERE

By car: From Assisi take S75 to Foligno, then S316 toward Montefalco (approximately 22 miles from Assisi).
By public transport: Bus from Foligno is the best way to reach Montefalco via public vehicle.

WHERE TO STAY

Montefalco is best visited as a daytrip from Assisi or check out: *Casa San Fortunato* (tel. 0742-790-102).

TOURIST OFFICE

There is no tourist office in Montefalco. Try the Umbrian region office in Perugia, *Assessorato al Turismo-Regione dell'Umbria,* C. so Vannucci, 30, 06100 Perugia (tel. 075-5041), or the tourist office in Assisi may be of some help.

NOTES

St. Clare of the Cross, patron saint of Montefalco, has her Feast Day on August 17. In addition to the sanctuary, the quiet medieval village of Montefalco has an excellent collection of paintings. The ex-church of San Francesco on Via Ringhiera Umbra (off the central Piazza del Commune) houses a large group including superb Renaissance frescos of the life of Saint Francis (open 9am-noon and 3:30-6:30pm, closed Sun.; L2000 entrance fee).

MONTEPULCIANO

Preserved Medieval Town of St. Agnes

Except ye see signs and wonders
ye will not believe.

—John 4:48

When Catherine of Siena went on pilgrimage to the shrine of St. Agnes in Montepulciano, she knelt to kiss the feet of the incorrupt body of the saint. Suddenly, the foot of St. Agnes jerked away, preventing her sister saint from humbling herself.

On a second visit, Catherine, determined to avoid a repeat of the first incident, went to the head of St. Agnes and prayed. Soon, the many visitors to the shrine saw white cross-shaped particles falling like snow around St. Agnes and St. Catherine. During her lifetime, miraculous white spiritual rays had frequently descended around St. Agnes while she was in ecstasies.

St. Agnes was born in Montepulciano in 1268. At age nine, she joined a group of holy women called the Sisters of the Sack because of the rough cloth they wore. At fifteen, with special Papal permission, she became an abbess of a convent near Orvieto. Her austere life was filled with miraculous materializations of food for the convent, fulfilled prophecies and levitations.

The citizens of Montepulciano built St. Agnes a new monastery in the town at a site which had been a house of prostitution. St. Agnes remained abbess of the monastery until her death at age forty-nine. Her partially incorrupt body is still in the monastery church in the delightful Tuscan hilltop town of Montepulciano.

We and God have business with each other;
and in opening ourselves to His influence
our deepest destiny is fulfilled...

—William James

Montepulciano

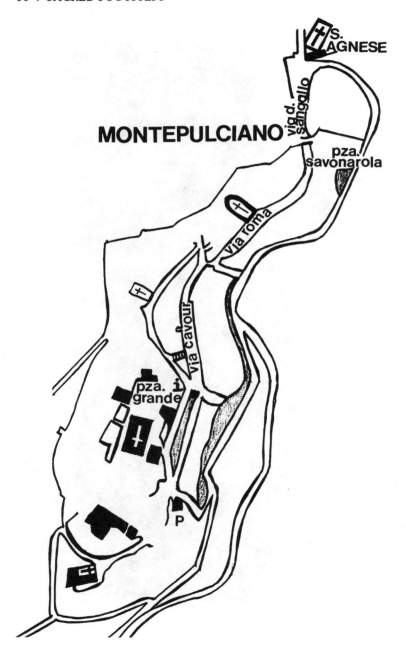

MONTEPULCIANO
REGION: TUSCANY   PROVINCE: SIENA

WHAT TO SEE

The Sanctuary of St. Agnes (Sanctuario di S. Agnese).
Open: Mornings and afternoons, daily.

The partially incorrupt body of St. Agnes is in a marble urn at the center of the main altar. The cell where she lived the last eleven years of her life, and where her body was exposed incorrupt for 270 years, is through a doorway to the right of the pulpit.

HOW TO GET THERE

By car: Montepulciano is easily reachable as a daytrip from either Assisi (approximately 55 miles) or Siena (approximately 42 miles). From Autostrade 1 exit either Chianciana (S146) or Bettolle (S327). Cars are not allowed within Montepulciano, a preserved medieval city. The Sanctuary and lodging are at the north end of the town walls at the junction of the roads toward Bettolle/Al, Pienza/Siena and Chianciano. Park outside the gate near Piazza Savonarola.

By public transport: Train, Station Chiusi (8 1/2 miles from Montepulciano). Buses run frequently from the Chiusi Station to town. The train station at Montepulciano is only a stop for slow local trains. Buses to Montepulciano are available from Siena and Florence.

WHERE TO STAY

Pilgrim accommodations are scant in Montepulclano. It's best as a daytrip from Assisi or Siena or stay in a hotel near the Sanctuary:
Albergo "Il Marzocco," Piazza Savonarola 18 (tel. 0578-757-262). Approximately L33,000 per person for room with bath. Also, the tourist office has a list of homes which rent private rooms.

TOURIST OFFICE

AAST, Via Ricci 9 (tel. 0578-757-442). The tourist office is located at the opposite end of town from the Sanctuary and hotel off the main town plaza, Piazza Grande. Open: mornings and afternoons, daily.

NOTES

St. Agnes' Feast Day is April 20. Montepulciano, the highest Tuscan hilltown at 2000 feet, is set amid delightful walking country. Hot springs nearby at Bagno Vignoni still offer sulfur cures which were once taken by St. Catherine of Siena.

IX

ITALY

SAN GIOVANNI ROTONDO

The Prophet of Gargano -
Padre Pio

*I shall be able to do much more for you when I am in Heaven
than I can while I am on earth.*

—Padre Pio

A million pilgrims a year visit the small town of San
Giovanni Rotondo on the southern Italian peninsula of
Gargano. They seek the living presence of a man called the
Second St. Francis, a man who died there in 1968.

Francesco Forgione was born near Naples in 1887. At
age ten, he wanted to be a friar who wore a beard and a
hood, a Capuchin. His father, a poor farmer, went to
America to earn money for his son's schooling. Though not
a brilliant scholar, the boy was accepted into a Capuchin
Friary at age sixteen.

One night while praying in the Friary, Francesco, now
called Pio, suddenly found his consciousness transferred to
the home of a wealthy man who was dying. At the same
moment the man's wife was giving birth to their child, a
baby girl. The Virgin Mary appeared to Pio and said he
was to be the child's spiritual guardian. Pio protested that
he wasn't even a priest yet; the Divine Mother reassured
him and said She would send the child to him later.

Pio wrote a report of his experience and gave it to his
superiors; they promptly filed away the possible halluci-
nation or dream.

Seventeen years later in 1922 a troubled teenage girl
named Giovanna went with a friend to confession at St.
Peter's Basilica in Rome. "All priests are gone for the day,"
a guard told them. Leaving, they met a Capuchin priest

who heard Giovanna's confession. Padre Pio was the priest who heard her confession though he never left San Giovanni Rotondo (about 230 miles from Rome) from 1916 until his death in 1968.

The following year Giovanna went with her aunt to see a famous priest named Padre Pio in San Giovanni Rotondo. To her surprise, he welcomed her by name and exclaimed that he knew her. Giovanna said that they hadn't met. Then, he revealed that she was born on the day her father died and that he had heard her confession in St. Peter's the year before.

Bilocation was only one of Padre Pio's many miraculous charisms. In 1910, when he was ordained a priest, he offered himself to God as a "victim soul," one who willingly suffers for the sins of others. Within a year, small sore red spots appeared on his palms and soles of his feet. Padre Pio hid these marks from all but his confessor.

In 1918, the sores began to flow blood. Even atheist doctors, among the many that examined Padre Pio, could not heal or explain the sacred wounds. Padre Pio, embarrassed by the stigmata, received special permission to cover his palms with fingerless gloves.

Padre Pio healed many hopeless medical cases through a variety of miraculous interventions and prayers. Often he would be at the Friary and simultaneously appear at the bedside of the sufferer. He might touch or slap the sufferer or command him to get up (out of a coma). His bilocation was usually accompanied by a distinct perfume odor which was also recognizable when in his physical presence at the Friary. He always said that he had no power to heal; that all he could do was pray that God's will be done.

During World War II, Allied bombers reported seeing the apparition of a monk just before mechanical failures prevented them from bombing San Giovanni Rotondo.

Numerous documents attest to his clairvoyant powers; people whose confessions he heard said he knew things about them that they had never told anyone.

In 1940 he enlisted the help of several talented physicians to build a Home for the Relief of Suffering in San Giovanni Rotondo. He disliked the word hospital which represented a place of horror and suffering to him. His vision was a place where physicians and other healthcare professionals, working as instruments of God, practiced in a spiritually aware way with medically advanced technology; he believed this combination would create the highest curative environment. His Home succeeded in fulfilling this mission and continues to relieve the suffering of many patients who come to San Giovanni Rotondo.

Shortly before his death at age eighty-one, the "Prophet of Gargano" was questioned about his appearances in various other places despite having never left San Giovanni Rotondo. He said, *"'whether it's true or not that I am found in various places by bilocation, trilocation or whatever, you must ask God and not me. All I can tell you is that I always try to remain attached to the thread of His will. For this reason, I am always where I am.'"*[7]

Padre Pio

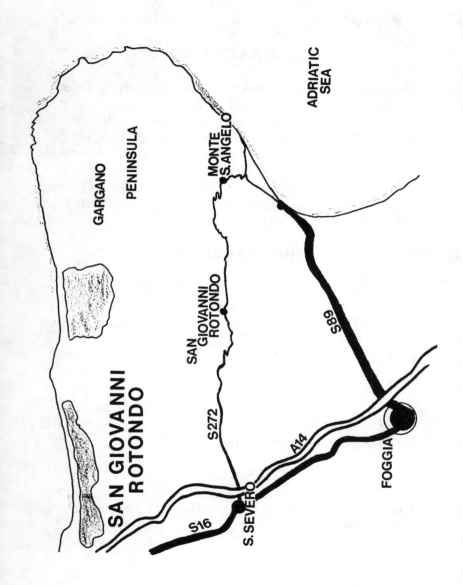

SAN GIOVANNI ROTONDO
REGION: PUGLIA   PROVINCE: FOGGIA

WHAT TO SEE

Our Lady of Grace Church (Santa Maria delle Grazie).
Open: Mornings and afternoons, daily.

    To the left of the Church is preserved the original smaller Church where Padre Pio conducted Mass. Upstairs in the choir, in 1918, he received the stigmata. *The Crypt* under the newer Church contains Padre Pio's tomb.

The Cell of Padre Pio is preserved in the Friary. Pictorial displays of his life are in the passageways which leads from the Church to his Cell.

HOW TO GET THERE

By car: Autostrade A14, exit at San Severo and follow the signs to San Giovanni Rotondo.

By public transport: Train (from Foggia), Station Manfredonia, about 24 miles from San Giovanni. SITA buses run approximately 14 times a day to San Giovanni.

WHERE TO STAY

Hotel Santa Maria delle Grazie, Piazza San Pio 5, 71013 San Giovanni Rotondo (tel. 0882-853-831).

TOURIST OFFICE

There is an information desk, staffed by Capuchin monks, in the Church.

NOTES

Canonization of saints can take centuries; Padre Pio has not been given a Feast Day yet. The Gargano Peninsula, projecting like a spur from the boot of Italy, is one of Italy's most attractive natural regions. Near San Giovanni Rotondo is Mont St. Angelo, a site recommended to pilgrims by Padre Pio. Here in the 5th century the Archangel St. Michael reportedly appeared.

X

ITALY

SUBIACO

Twin Brother and Sister Saints -
Saint Benedict & Saint Scholastica

Ora et labora
Pray and work

—St. Benedict

St. Scholastica and St. Benedict were twins born in Norcia, Italy in 480 A.D. They died sixty-three years later, within a short time of each other, and were buried in the same tomb. Benedict, the father of Western monasticism, and Scholastica, the first abbess, left a powerful spiritual imprint on Subiaco where they founded many monasteries.

Little is known of the twins' childhoods except that their parents were prosperous. Benedict studied in Rome and at age twenty became disillusioned with the decadence of Roman life. Driven by a desire to know and serve God, he renounced a promising career and journeyed fifty miles inland from Rome to the woods of Mount Taleo, now called Subiaco, overlooking a beautiful valley. There he met a hermit who lived above a grotto. The hermit occasionally lowered food to him in a basket during the three years Benedict lived in seclusion in a cave.

After this period, Benedict began to preach and attracted followers who asked him to be their abbot. Eventually, however, his monks found Benedict's standards too high and they tried to poison him. As he was handed the goblet of lethal wine, Benedict blessed it and the cup immediately shattered. A cadre of harlots also were sent to Benedict's dwelling in an unsuccessful effort to debauch his holy life.

Later, Benedict went south to Montecassino and built a monastery over a Roman temple which had been dedicated to the god Mercury. It became the motherhouse of his Order. At this site he wrote the famous rules which became the basis for Western monastic life.

Unfortunately, there is little recorded about the life of Benedict's twin sister, St. Scholastica. One of the few events known about her occurred at Montecassino. She and Benedict would meet at a house near their monasteries. On the last of these visits, Scholastica, realizing her death was near, asked Benedict to stay the night so that they could "keep on talking about the joys of heaven till morning."[8] Benedict declined; Scholastica began intense prayer. Soon, the clear skies were darkened; there was a sudden burst of thunder, lightening and a downpour which made Benedict's departure impossible. Scholastica died three days later. Benedict, by then back at his abbey, knew of her death because he saw her soul, in the form of a dove, fly to heaven.

Another of his visions occurred soon after his sister's death when "in the dead of the night he suddenly beheld a flood of light shining down from above, more brilliant than the sun... the whole world was gathered before his eyes in what appeared to be a single ray of light."[9]

Benedict died within a short time and was buried with Scholastica "just as in life their souls had always been one in God".[10] The exalting vibrations of Subiaco make it an ideal site to

... contemplate with our inner eye the mirror of God's wisdom, where all things shine and are illumined.

—Ruysbroeck

St. Benedict and St. Scholastica - last meal

St. Benedict sees his sister's soul ascend

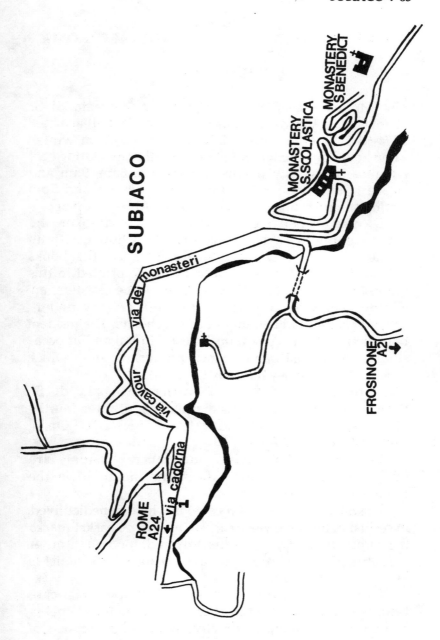

SUBIACO

REGION: LAZIO **PROVINCE: ROMA**

WHAT TO SEE

The Monastery of Saint Scholastica (Abbazia di S. Scholastica), Via dei Monasteri, 15, 00028 Subiaco (tel. 0774-85-525). Open: 9am-12:30pm and 4-6:45pm winter; same hours in summer except open until 8pm. During ceremonies (Feast Day masses are at 7am, 8am, 9am and 10:30am; and, Vespers at 4pm during winter and 5pm during summer) only the Church in the Abbey is open.

Located about two miles outside town overlooking the Aniene gorge, the Abbey has a Gothic Church with an eighteenth century Church built around it. The first books printed in Europe outside Germany were printed in this monastery in 1465-67. There also are three cloisters, an eleventh century campanile, a fifteenth century underground chapel, and a library open to scholars. The resident Benedictine monks give tours (mostly in Italian but occasionally in English) and operate a pilgrim's shop which sells herbs and honey made by the monks.

The Monastery of Saint Benedict (Abbazia di S. Benedetto). On the same road, uphill about three-fourths of a mile from St. Scholastica's (tel. 0777-85-039). Open: 9am-12:30pm and 3-6pm.

Two frescoed churches and several chapels are uniquely carved into the side of the mountain in the remote woods of Mt. Taleo.

The *Sacro Speco* (sacred cave) is where Benedict lived in seclusion for three years early in his life. A basket marks the spot where St. Romulus lowered food to him. A perpetual flame burns in the cave because St. Benedict is Europe's Patron Saint.

To the right of the Sacro Speco is a spiral staircase leading to the *Chapel of St. Gregory*. Inside the chapel is displayed a stunningly attractive fresco of St. Francis of

Assisi. It was completed shortly after his pilgrimage to Subiaco, and is thought to be the earliest, most accurate rendering of St. Francis. The Chapel is usually locked but the monk who is almost always present in the area may open it for you.

Near St. Gregory's Chapel is the *Grotto of the Shepherds* where St. Benedict preached. A terrace just beyond the grotto looks out over the wild valley. A *Holy Rose Tree* against which St. Benedict apparently threw himself to resist temptation can be seen from this site.

HOW TO GET THERE

By car: Autostrade A24 (direction Pescara) from Rome, about 46 miles. Exit Mandela. Follow signs to Subiaco. The monasteries are just outside town (see map).
By public transport: Subiaco is about a two hour bus trip from Rome. Buses leave from Rome's Viale Castro Pretoria (or bus from Tivoli).

WHERE TO STAY

The Abbey of St. Scholastica does, on occasion, accept men desiring accommodations in a spiritual atmosphere. Women pilgrims may be accepted at the *Casa di Priegh* if space is available. The Casa is a small community of sisters residing in rustic dwellings above the Monastery of Saint Benedict. It is a steep walk (approximately twenty minutes) up a stony road to reach the Casa which is located at the lovely site where the hermit St. Romulus lowered food to St. Benedict. Inquire at St. Scholastica's Abbey.

TOURIST OFFICE

AAST, Via Cadorna n. 59 (tel. 0774-85-397).
Open: Mon. 8am-2pm; Tues.-Sat. 8am-2pm and 3:30-7:30pm; Sun. 9am-noon.

NOTES

July 11 is St. Benedict's Feast Day; St. Scholastica's is February 10. Beautiful Gregorian chants are sung as part of the Benedictine Mass at Subiaco.

XI
ITALY

LORETO

The Miraculous Holy House

And the angel said unto her, Fear not, Mary: for thou hast found favor with God. And behold, thou shalt conceive in thy womb, and bring forth a son, and shalt call his name Jesus.
—The Annunciation, Luke 1:30

The Holy House in Nazareth is where the angel Gabriel announced to Mary that she would become the mother of Jesus. The house was protected in the third century by Saint Helen, Empress of Constantinople, who built a small church around it. Mysteriously, in the thirteenth century, as Moslems threatened to overrun the Holy Land, the House reportedly disappeared. In 1291, it was rediscovered near Yugoslavia. When Moslems invaded Yugoslavia three years later, the House vanished again, only to reappear soon after in a grove of laurels called Loreto.

The earliest legends of the House's strange travels included transport by angels. Recent archeological excavations, however, support the theory that the House was transported by ship to Italy.

St. Francis de Sales, Galileo, Descartes, St. Ignatius Loyola and Mozart were among the many millions of pilgrims who journeyed to Loreto. St. Thérèse of Lisieux on her visit to the Holy House explained its humbleness by saying that "Jesus is content to show us His home so as to make us love poverty and the hidden life."11

On the altar in the tiny house is the most copied Madonna in the world - the Black Virgin of Loreto. She is usually adorned in traditional dress of the region. Because of the legend of the flying Holy House, the Loreto Madonna is the patron saint of aviators. Charles Lindberg carried an image of Her on his 1927 Atlantic flight and the Apollo 9 crew were accompanied on their moon flight by a medallion inscribed with the image of this Queen of Angels.

...Mother of divine grace...morning star...
Mystical rose...Ark of the Covenant...
Seat of wisdom...Queen of Prophets, pray for us...
—Portion of the Litany of Loreto

The Black Madonna of Loreto

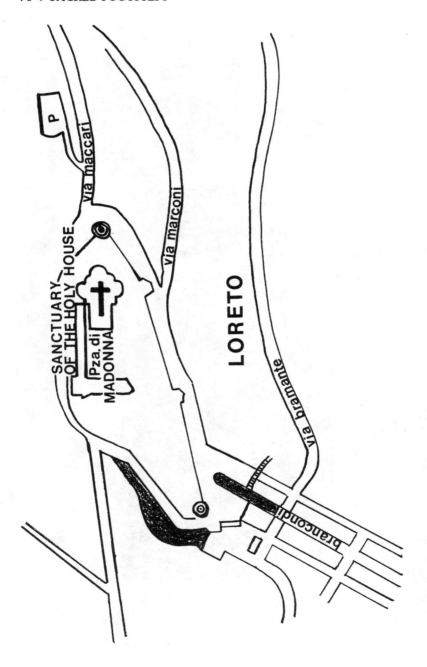

LORETO
REGION: MARCHE   PROVINCE: ANCONA

WHAT TO SEE

Sanctuary of the Holy House (Santuario della Santa Casa), Piazza della Madonna, 60025 Loreto (tel. 071-970-104). Open: Mornings and afternoons, daily.

"Tremble all you who enter here, because this is the holiest place on earth" is inscribed over the door of the House of Loreto. Construction of a large Basilica around the Holy House began in 1468 and ended in the eighteenth century. The Basilica contains numerous chapels and frescos.

HOW TO GET THERE

By car: Loreto is just off Autostrade A14 , about 15 miles south of Ancona. The exit and signs directing motorists to the small town are well marked.

By public transport: Train, Station Loreto. Easily reached from Ancona. The station is not in town but connected to it by bus.

WHERE TO STAY

Instituto Immacolata Concezione, Via Maccari 137, 60025 Loreto (tel. 071-977-143).

If this pilgrim's house is full, there are numerous others in Loreto such as *Instituto Orsoline di Gesu* (tel. 071-970-192) and *Suore S. Famiglia di Nazareth* (tel. 071-970-181).

TOURIST OFFICE

AAST, Via Solari 3. Open: Mon.-Fri. 8am-1:30pm and 4-8pm; Sun. 9am-noon.

NOTES

Loreto is usually filled with thousands of pilgrims on August 15 (Assumption Day celebrating the Blessed Virgin Mary's ascension into Heaven) and September 8 (celebrated as her birthday). Also, a popular pilgrimage day is December 10, the Translation of the Santa Casa (Holy House). Many trains carrying the sick and injured arrive in Loreto during these holy days.

XII
FRANCE

PARIS

Visions of the Lady of the Sun -
St. Catherine Labouré

And a great portent appeared in heaven, a woman clothed with the sun, and the moon under her feet and on her head a crown of twelve stars...

—Apocalypse 12:1

One night in 1830 a young nun lay sleeping at her convent in Paris. "Sister Labouré" a voice called to her. "Sister Labouré," it repeated. Catherine Labouré awoke and was startled to see a small child at her bedside. "Come to the chapel at once," he said, "the Blessed Virgin awaits you."

Not sure if she was dreaming, Catherine got out of bed and followed the small figure towards the chapel. For many years, she had longed to see the Divine Mother with her own eyes. This desire now overpowered the disbelief she felt as she walked behind the angelic stranger. Still, she hoped her superiors would not see her wandering the halls at this hour of the night!

Entering the chapel, she was shocked to see all the candles lit. She heard a curious sound like the rustle of silk just as the small child announced, "Here is the Blessed Virgin." Catherine stood transfixed; it was as though the light of a thousand suns dazzled from the Beautiful Lady before her.

"My child," said the Lady, "the good God wishes to charge you with a mission...you will see certain things...you will be contradicted, but do not fear...tell with confidence all that passes within you [to your spiritual director]. "12

The Lady then began to speak of the abundance of sorrow and danger that would come upon France and the world because they had forgotten God. Specifically, she predicted that the next forty years would be full of misery for France. After two hours of conversing with the Lady of the Sun, Catherine saw her "fade away and became but a shadow, which moved toward the tribune, the way she had come."[13] The French Revolution of 1830 erupted a week after the Lady's appearance.

Four months after this first apparition, Catherine was again in the chapel at the convent on rue du Bac. This time she was with her sisters at evening prayers. Suddenly, she heard that sound: A noise like the faint rustling of a silk gown. Looking towards the altar, she saw the Lady of the Sun. The Lady was standing on a globe and in her hands she held a globe. Rings on her hands were set with precious stones and resplendent rays streamed from these gems. The Lady said, "these rays symbolize the graces I shed upon those who ask. The gems from which rays do not fall are the graces for which souls forget to ask."[14]

Suddenly an oval frame formed around the Lady with the words "O Mary, conceived without sin, pray for us who have recourse to thee." The image then seemed to revolve and on the reverse Catherine saw a large M surmounted by a bar and a cross. Beneath the M were the hearts of Jesus and Mary, the one crowned with thorns, and the other pierced with a sword. Twelve stars encircled the whole.

The Lady said, "have a medal struck of this model. All who wear it will receive great graces..."[15] Catherine had this vision once more. During the last vision, the Lady said, "you will see me no more, but you will hear my voice in your prayers."[16]

Following the visions, Catherine struggled to convince her confessor to cast a medal of the image she had seen. Finally in 1832, he consented to have the image made into a medal. He also agreed to keep secret Catherine's identity as the nun who had seen the apparition.

The medal quickly became popular. Its formal name was forgotten and it was called the "miraculous medal" because immense numbers of healings and religious conversions were attributed to it. Seven million copies of the medal were sold in four years despite the strong anti-religious sentiment in France at the time.

Catherine completed her novitiate training at the convent and was assigned to work in a home for the aged operated by the nuns of her Order. Eventually, word leaked (from her confessor) that a nun at rue du Bac had seen the vision of the miraculous medal. Despite conjecture that Catherine was this visionary, she kept her identity as this nun hidden for forty-six years. She lived a life of humble service, her spiritual stature unrevealed.

Toward the end of her life, Catherine found herself in a quandary: Her confessor had died and a statue the Lady had requested of Herself had not been made.

Catherine had to go to her superior and reveal her secret in order to complete this last mission. In 1876, after Catherine's death at age seventy, her superior disclosed that Catherine Labouré was the nun who had seen the Lady of the Sun and the vision of the miraculous medal.

The appearance in 1830 of the Lady of the Sun in Paris began the "Marian Age," an era in which numerous appearances have been credited to the Divine Mother. Today, through visionaries' reports in Medjugorje, Yugoslavia and other places, the Queen of Peace apparently continues her call to mankind to banish world and individual suffering by turning to God. Coincidentally, the European Community has chosen a symbol of this "Age of Mary" to represent their unity - twelve stars in a circle like the twelve stars that surrounded Catherine's vision of the Lady.

In 1938, Catherine Labouré's body was uncovered and found incorrupt. During her life, Catherine once overheard a nun tell another that the sister who saw the Lady saw only a picture. "'*Sister...,*' replied Catherine, '*the sister who saw the Blessed Virgin saw her in flesh and bone, even as you and I see each other now .*'" 17

St. Catherine Labouré

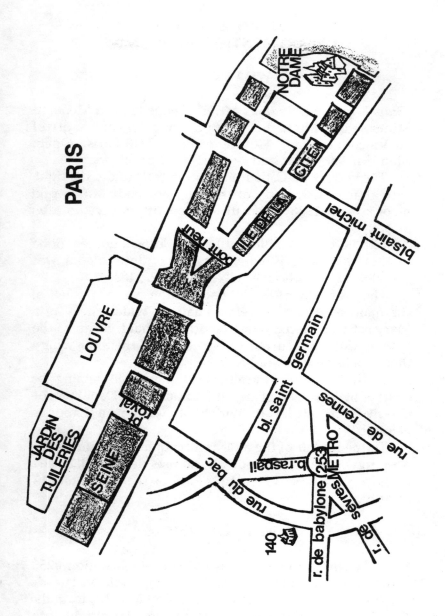

PARIS
REGION: CENTER
DEPARTMENT: VILLE DE PARIS

WHAT TO SEE

Chapel of the Miraculous Medal (Chapelle de la Médaille Miraculeuse), Motherhouse of the Daughters of Charity of St. Vincent de Paul, 140 rue du Bac, 75340 Paris. Open: Mon.-Sat. 9am-noon and 3-6pm; Sun. 10am-noon.

The body of St. Catherine Labouré rests under the right side altar of Our Lady of the Sun; her body was found incorrupt in 1938 when uncovered fifty-six years after burial.

The statue of the Blessed Lady holding a golden globe in the right altar is where the miraculous medal was revealed to St. Catherine on November 27, 1830.

The exact site of the first apparition was to the left of the main altar; a blue velvet chair on which the Virgin Mary sat was placed there. Another radiant vision of the Divine Mother occurred in the center of the altar where there is a large statue of her.

To the far right of the altar is a reliquary containing the heart of St. Vincent de Paul, co-founder of the Daughters of Charity (the Order to which St. Catherine Labouré belonged).

To the far left of the altar is a reliquary containing the wax figure and bones of St. Louise de Marillac, co-foundress with St. Vincent de Paul of the Daughters of Charity.

HOW TO GET THERE

Take the Metro to the Sévres-Bablone stop (station #253 which is on the Left Bank). Walk one block on rue de Babylone. A large department store, Bon Marché, is on the corner of rue du Bac and rue du Babylone. Turn right onto rue du Bac. 140 rue the Bac is on the left within the first block. There is also a rue du Bac Metro stop but it is a longer distance from the Motherhouse.

WHERE TO STAY

Prieuré Saint-Benoit-Saint Scholastique - Bénédictines du Sacré Coeur de Montmartre, 3-7, cité du Sacré-Coeur, 40 rue du Chevalier-de-la-Barre, 75018 Paris (tel. 1-46-06-14-71).

This Benedictine monastic community is located on Montmartre near the famous Sacré Coeur Basilica. The community emphatically requests pilgrims only, no tourists. The community rents out 25 single rooms, 40 rooms with 2 beds, and dormitories. Book at least one month in advance. When you write or call to reserve a room, ask for directions to the monastery.

If full, try the *Hôtel du Vieux Paris* 9 rue Git le Coeur, 75006 Paris (tel 1-43-54-41-66). It is located in the Latin quarter near Metro stop Saint Michel on a tiny street where Henry IV said "Here lives my heart" (his mistress resided here). The hotel is in a building constructed in about 1480. During the 1950's and early 60's "Beat Generation" poets and artists like Allen Ginsburg made the hotel their Paris home. It is indeed a unique experience staying at this hotel, yet the location is good for visiting rue du Bac and Paris Cathedrals and it is inexpensive by Paris standards. Approximately, a 200F singles; 250F doubles includes breakfast. (A recent note: The hotel is being remodeled and prices are expected to increase as a result.)

TOURIST OFFICE

Office du Tourisme, 127 Avenue des Champs-Elysees, 75008 Paris (tel. 47-23-61-72). Open: 9am-8pm daily except Christmas and New Year's Day. Metro stop is Charles-de-Gaulle-Étoile.

NOTES

November 28 is St. Catherine's Feast Day. The rue du Bac chapel is visited by many pilgrims. Wear earplugs if you wish to diminish the noise of the constant traffic! Don't be shocked by the vending machines which distribute miraculous medals for a small fee.

Paris is most joyous to visit in early spring or late fall when tourist throngs recede somewhat. A delightful way to experience both spectacular music and stunning church architecture is to attend some of the numerous concerts held regularly in Cathedrals such as Notre-Dame, St. Chapelle and St.-Germaine des Prés.

On the principal holidays honoring the Blessed Virgin Mary (Marian holidays) celebrations are held at all of France's Notre Dame (Our Lady) churches. These holidays are on March 25 (Annunciation Day which marks the announcing of the birth of Lord Jesus by the angel Gabriel to Mary); July 1 (the Visitation of Mary to her cousin Elizabeth with news of her miraculous conception); August 15 (Assumption Day celebrated as the date of Mary's ascension into Heaven); and September 8 (the Nativity of the Blessed Virgin Mary).

CHARTRES

Ancient Spiritual Magnet

Over all things, under all things
Outside all, inside all
Within, but not enclosed
Without, but not excluded
Above, but not raised up
Below, but not suppressed
Wholly above, presiding
Wholly beneath, sustaining
Wholly without, embracing
Wholly within, fulfilling.
—Hildebert of Lemans, *Super Cuncta*

The vast treasures of famed Chartres Cathedral hint at a cosmic eternality. The ancient holy site, supposedly the sacred capital of the Druids, priests and priestesses of the Celts, was a medieval spiritual magnet. Beneath its famous cathedral, geobiologists recently have discovered fourteen water channels which converge at a single point under the choir. When measured by scientific instruments, the intensity of vibrations at this spot is as high as that found in some Tibetan monasteries and Egyptian pyramids.18

Hidden in a sea of chairs in the Cathedral's nave is a large Labyrinth, the mandala-like metaphor of the pilgrimage of life. The Labyrinth is a design of stones laid into the paved floor. It was traversed by medieval pilgrims on their knees or in dance. Electromagnetic intensities in the center of the Labyrinth match heights (in bliss states) recorded of human consciousness, yet, just before entering the centerpoint, the measurements mimic near-death body states. It seems that the initiates needed to symbolically experience death before escaping the Labyrinth's maze and entering its celestial promise.

Chartres' Cathedral is full of mysteries, as if its diaphanous pools of ruby, emerald and opal light, reflecting from its stained glass windows aren't enough to beguile tourist and pilgrim alike. Beneath its floor is the largest crypt in France. It contains numerous chapels and a well which was the focus of Druid ceremonies. Adjacent to the well is the Chapel of the Black Virgin of the Underground. This Black Madonna is linked magically to a pre-Christian tradition of a Virgin who would bring forth a child.

Upstairs, there is a second dark Virgin, the Virgin of the Pillar. Candles and devotees abound before her shrine. On special holy days, another Chartres treasure is displayed before her, the Sancta Camisa, a veil supposedly worn by the Virgin Mary. The veil was given to Charlemagne by the Empress Helen of Constantine, a preserver of holy artifacts. Chartres obtained it in 876 from Charles the Bald, Charlemagne's grandson.

During a battle in the Middle Ages, Chartres' citizens waved the holy veil from the city's ramparts. Seeing it, weary Chartres troops rallied to repulse an invading army. The veil is still carried through the streets of Chartres in a procession every August 15th (Assumption Day).

Chartres is understandably a tourist mecca so go early in the day to the Cathedral or consider wearing earplugs. Wander through Chartres' picturesque side streets and canals; there are undiscovered churches and in spring, radiant tulip and pansy gardens. This ancient spiritual magnet has the power to draw the pilgrims' consciousness heavenward so that...

...We are elaborated beyond our personality, and transformed up to the immersion of love, where we possess bliss and are one with God.

—Ruysbroeck

Canal of Chartres

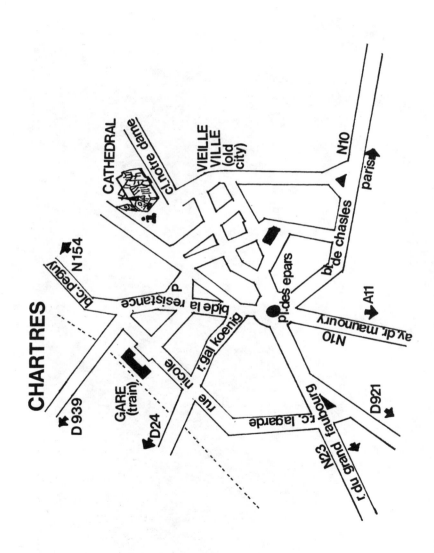

CHARTRES
REGION: CENTER
DEPARTMENT: EURE-ET-LOIRE

Cathedral of Our Lady of Chartres (Cathédrale Notre Dame de Chartres), 11 rue des Lisses, 28000 Chartres (tel. 37-21-32-33). Open: Daily, 7:30am-7:30pm; Oct.-Mar. 7:30am-7:00pm.

The Labyrinth (Labyrinthe) is on the floor of the nave soon after entering the main doors. *Our Lady of the Pillar* (Notre Dame du Pilier) is on the north side (left) of the Cathedral.

The Shroud of the Virgin Mary (Sancta Camisa) is displayed daily in the Treasury. Open: Mon.-Sat., 10am-noon and 3-6pm; Sun. 2-6pm. Oct.-Dec., Mon.-Sat., 10am-noon and 2-6pm; Sun. 2-5pm. Feb.-Apr., Mon.-Sat., 10am-noon and 2:30-5pm; Sun. 2:30-5pm. Admission free.

The *crypt* contains the Druid well, numerous chapels and the *Chapel of Our Lady of the Underground* (Notre Dame de Souterre). Open: Daily by tour usually at 11am, 2:15pm, 3:30pm, 4:30pm and in July and August, 5:15pm. For tickets, approximately 7F, go to the shop called "La Crypte," 18 Cloître Notre Dame, at the end of the street on the right side of the Cathedral (south portal). Also, there are Masses in the Chapel of Our Lady of the Underground and at those times a door which leads from the outside to the Chapel is open near the north portal.

HOW TO GET THERE

By car: Autoroute A10/11 from Paris, approximately 60 miles.

By public transport: There are frequent trains from Gare Montparnasse in Paris direct to Chartres, approximately 50-80 minutes. Lines Paris/Le Mans, Rennes or Nantes. The Chartres train station is within walking distance of the Cathedral and old city.

WHERE TO STAY

Chartres is an easy daytrip from Paris or stay at:
L'accueil de Pèlerins de Chartres, 8, rue du Fosse Bourg Jouy, 28300 Mainvilliers (tel. 37-22-24-44). 5 1/2 miles from Chartres on route D24. Mostly dormitories.

TOURIST OFFICE

Office du Tourisme, 7 Cloître Notre-Dame, 28000 Chartres. Located in a building to the left of the Cathedral's main portal. Open: Mornings and afternoons.*

NOTES

Students still walk from Paris to Chartres on pilgrimage during Pentecost (late April or May) which commemorates the descent of the Holy Spirit on the Apostles. Also, there are celebrations on the holy days of August 15 and September 8. During July and August, Chartres hosts festivals of religious music.

National holidays in France are January 1; Shrove Tuesday (The Tuesday before Ash Wednesday which is the Wednesday preceding Easter Sunday), Good Friday; Easter; May 1 (Labor Day); Ascension Day (40 days after Easter), Whit Monday; July 14 (Bastille Day); August 15 (Assumption Day); November 1 (All Saints Day); November 11 (Armistice Day); and December 25. Most businesses and shops are closed on these days.

---

* Generally, in France, "open mornings and afternoons" means 9am-noon and 2-6pm.

FRANCE

LOURDES

Appearance of the Beautiful Lady - St. Bernadette

Go and drink in the spring and wash there...
—The Beautiful Lady to Bernadette Soubirous

Fourteen year old Bernadette Soubirous, obeying the request of a Lady only she could see, scratched at dry ground and smeared dirt on her face. Many witnesses of the girl's bizarre actions were convinced she was a lunatic or a fraud.

Yet soon after, on the spot where Bernadette dug, a spring appeared where none had existed. A Lourdes mother, distraught over the doctor's pronouncement of no hope for her dying child, rushed to the spring and immersed her paralytic son in its waters. His recovery was immediate and medically unexplainable; thus in 1858 began the claim of the miraculous healing waters of Lourdes. Today, voluminous reports of Lourdes cures continue to baffle skeptical medical scientists.

Initially, both secular and religious authorities tried to discredit Bernadette's visions of a "Beautiful Lady" in the Massabielle Grotto. She was put through a multitude of crude and crafty examinations in an effort to prove that she was a liar or insane. Because Bernadette was so obviously mentally stable and so innocent of guile, she passed these trials with a natural grace.

The chief ecclesiastic of Lourdes, however, refused to believe Bernadette until she conveyed to him the Lady's message: "I am the Immaculate Conception." He realized that these were words which Bernadette, so ignorant of Church dogma, could not possibly have fantasized. Soon, a formal Church commission began investigation of her story.

At her first appearance, the Beautiful Lady had asked Bernadette to come to the grotto seventeen more times. When these visits were over Bernadette assumed she would return to the simple life she led before the appearance of the Lady. Thousands of people seeking cures were pouring into Lourdes, however, and Bernadette was sought by many of them. She was sheltered for a time at the Hospice of the Sisters of Charity in Lourdes; still, her peaceful existence in her poor, loving family was gone. "'I cannot promise you happiness in this world only in the next,'"[19] the Lady had told Bernadette.

When it appeared that the commission's investigation would authenticate the appearance of the Blessed Virgin at Lourdes, Bernadette was advised by the Bishop to become a nun. Obediently she accepted this path for which she felt ill qualified - she was asthmatic, uneducated and viewed herself as worthless.

At age twenty-four, she was accepted into the Order of the Sisters of Charity and Christian Instruction. Shortly before she left Lourdes to live at their Motherhouse in Nevers, a chapel above the Massabielle Grotto was completed as requested by the Lady. Bernadette attended the opening ceremonies.

Bernadette's superiors at Nevers thought the celebrity joining their Order should be humbled; they assigned her kitchen duties. Bernadette, who never desired attention or rewards from her experience, sweetly and cheerfully accepted all humiliations. She lived at Nevers only twelve years, dying there at age thirty-six.

To doubters of her story she once said, *"'I did not ask you to believe it, I only told you what I had seen.'"*[20]

St. Bernadette

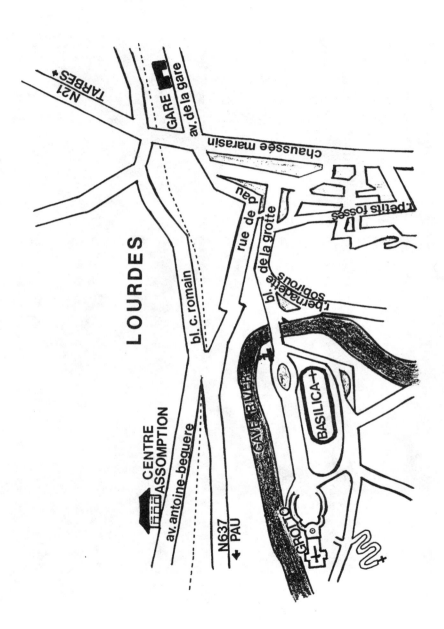

LOURDES
REGION: MIDI-PYRÉNÉES
DEPARTMENT: HAUT-PYRÉNÉES

WHAT TO SEE

The Grotto of Massabielle. Open: All year, all hours.

The Beautiful Lady appeared here to Saint Bernadette eighteen times in 1858. Within the outdoor grotto is the miraculous spring that welled up in the spot where the Lady told Bernadette to dig. The fountains adjacent to the grotto provide water from the spring for pilgrims to bottle and drink. The Baths alongside the grotto are not open for viewing, but both the healthy and sick can bathe in their waters.

The Basilica of the Immaculate Conception was built in the late 1800s in response to the Lady's request for a chapel. The chancel is located above the exact spot where she appeared.

The Crypt is a place for reflection and silence. St. Bernadette was present at the first Mass celebrated here in 1866. Her father was one of twenty-five men who cut out the main corridor of the crypt from the rock.

The Rosary Basilica was built only thirty years after the apparitions to honor the Lady who appeared with a rosary in her hand.

The Cachot (or "jail") on rue des Petits Fosses was the dwelling of Bernadette's family at the time of the apparitions: Lourdes. Open: Easter-Oct., 8am-7:30pm. Admission free.

Moulin de Boly, rue Bernadette Soubirous (tel. 62-94-23-53) is the birthplace of Saint Bernadette. The house is well marked. There is a small admission fee.

HOW TO GET THERE

By air: Lourdes has its own airport.
By car: Easily reached by following signs along the major routes from any direction.
By public transport: Train, Station Lourdes. Lines Paris/Bordeaux/Tarbes/Nice/Toulouse/Bayonne, etc.. Taxi to lodging.

WHERE TO STAY

Centre Assomption, 21, rue Antoine-Beguere, 65100 Lourdes, (tel. 62-94-39-81). Operated by the Religious of the Assumption. 90 rooms of 1 or 2 beds, showers near the rooms. Elevator, parking, chapel, garden. Some rooms with a view of the Massabielle Grotto and Basilicas which are within walking distance. By car, follow the signs through Lourdes toward Pau (route N637). Rue Antoine-Beguere forks to the right off route N637 just as you begin to see the Grotto and Basilica to your left. Price is approximately 130F (which includes full pension) per person plus a small membership fee.

TOURIST OFFICE

Office de Touristes et Isolés is under the right-hand ramp as you face the Basilica. Open: 9am-noon and 2-6pm.

NOTES

Lourdes, along with Jerusalem and Rome, is one of three Catholic world capitals of prayer. Ignore its commercial "Palaces of Rosaries" and focus on the innate mystical quality of the beautiful Pyrenean valley, where it is located, and the Massabielle Grotto.

Millions of pilgrims visit Lourdes each year, yet most don't know that within the sacred Massabielle Grotto is a small bench where you can sit in silence. The bench is adjacent to the spot where St. Bernadette dug and discovered the spring of miraculous waters.

From April through October, thousands of pilgrims march in a nightly candlelight procession including hundreds who are pushed in wheelchairs. Major celebrations are held on February 11, anniversary of the first apparition called the holy day of Our Lady of Lourdes, April 16, St. Bernadette's Feast Day; August 15, the Assumption of the Blessed Virgin Mary; and in October, when a Rosary Pilgrimage to Lourdes takes place.

NEVERS

St. Bernadette's Incorrupt Body

REGION: BURGUNDY   DEPARTMENT: NIEVRE

Nevers is often overlooked as a place of pilgrimage. Yet, the Convent of St. Gildard in Nevers where St. Bernadette lived the last nine years of her life, is full of her peace and love of God.

WHAT TO SEE

Chapel of the Convent (Chapel of St. Bernadette) Motherhouse of the Sisters of Charity and Christian Instruction, 34 rue St.-Gildard, 58000 Nevers (tel. 86-57-79-99). Open: 6:30am-7:30pm from early April through late October daily; other times of the year open mornings and afternoons only.

Beautiful blue light streams into the chapel where the body of St. Bernadette, which was found incorrupt when exhumed thirty years after her death and again when exhumed a second time ten years later, rests in a glass reliquary. The hands and face of the Saint's body are now coated with a covering of wax.

Grotto of Our Lady of Waters is in the courtyard of the Convent. It contains a stone from the grotto at Lourdes and a statue which St. Bernadette said was the one which most resembles the Beautiful Lady she saw at Lourdes.

A *Museum* which traces the life of St. Bernadette and includes the chair in which she died is in the Convent courtyard. Open: the same hours as the Chapel.

HOW TO GET THERE

By car: Route N7 leads to Nevers. The Convent is near a park called Parc Roger Salengro. There is parking on the streets alongside the Park.

By public transport: Train, Station Nevers. Lines Paris/Clermont-Ferrand and Nantes/Lyon. Trains from the Loire and Massif Central pass daily through Nevers to Dijon.

WHERE TO STAY

Convent Saint-Gildard, 34, rue St.-Gildard, 58000 Nevers (tel. 86-57-79-99). The Sisters of Charité et Christian L'Instruction of Nevers accept those who wish to "walk in the footsteps of St. Bernadette." Rooms available with one or two beds; showers separate. Parking. Reservations preferred fifteen days in advance.

TOURIST OFFICE

Office du Tourisme, 31 rue du Rempart (tel. 86-54-07-03). Open: Mon.-Sat., 9am-12:30 and 2-6:30pm.

NOTES

There are ceremonies in Nevers in preparation for Easter. The Feast Day of St. Bernadette is April 16.

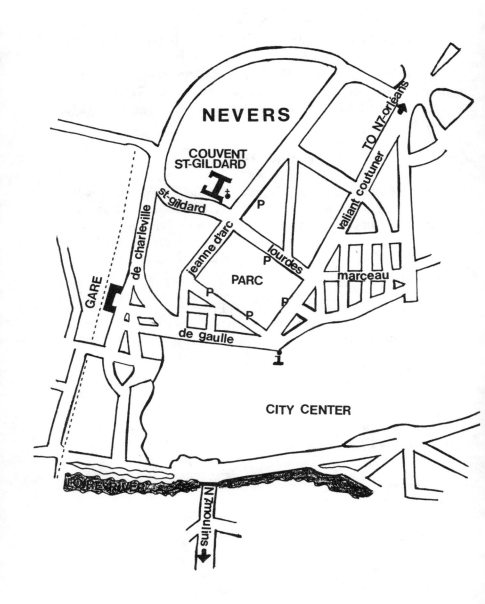

VÉZELAY
Pilgrimage to the Milky Way

"Priez pour nous à Compostelle"
Pray for us at Compostela
—Anonymous pilgrim refrain
from the Middle Ages

Streets once clamoring with the noise of pilgrims' fairs, marts and celebrations are quiet today in the charming little village of Vézelay. Its preserved ramparts and lofty Basilica evoke glory days when it was the center of tumultuous dramas.

In the Middle Ages, some of the bones of the then popular saint Mary Magdalene were thought to be safeguarded at Vézelay. As a result, the village became one of four main starting points for the famous pilgrimage to Santiago de Compostela in Spain. Compostela means field of stars and the holy pilgrimage was called the Milky Way.

Over many years, Vézelay flourished with illustrious people and events. In 1146, St. Bernard of Clairvaux preached the Second Crusade at Vézelay, as King Louis and Queen Eleanor of Aquitaine listened; in 1190, Richard the Lion-Hearted made peace with King Phillip of France there; and in 1217, St. Francis of Assisi chose Vézelay as the site of his first monastery in France. On a tragic note, one thousand pilgrims perished in 1120 in the large crypt of the Basilica of St. Mary Magdalene when fire swept through the sleeping quarters.

At the end of the thirteenth century, the discovery of the majority of St. Mary Magdalene's bones at St. Maximin in Provence, France brought changes to Vézelay: The pilgrimages diminished and the fairs and markets became less important.

Vézelay seemed to sleep through the next five centuries. It awoke somewhat in the nineteenth century when the magnificence of the Basilica of St. Mary Magdalene was recognized by the French Inspector of Historical Monuments. Restoration of the Basilica began in 1840 and was completed nineteen years later.

In the twentieth century, noted French author Romain Rolland, writer of "The Life of Sri Ramakrishna" and many other works, spent the last years of his life at 20 Grande-rue in Vézelay.

The beautiful setting and preserved medieval buildings of the village make it a jewel in the lush Burgundy countryside. Many tourists visit Vézelay in the summer but off-season it has few inhabitants. Its simplicity and quiet offer the retreatant a conducive place for the inner quest.

His Kingdom dwelleth in thee; lo! The riches of heaven are within thy soul, if thou be willing! Enter thou in and dwell in thine own self in the cleared ground of thine own mind and seek there the Kingdom. Enter thou in and dwell within thine own heart, for lo! There is God...

—Ephraim the Syrian

Street in Vézelay

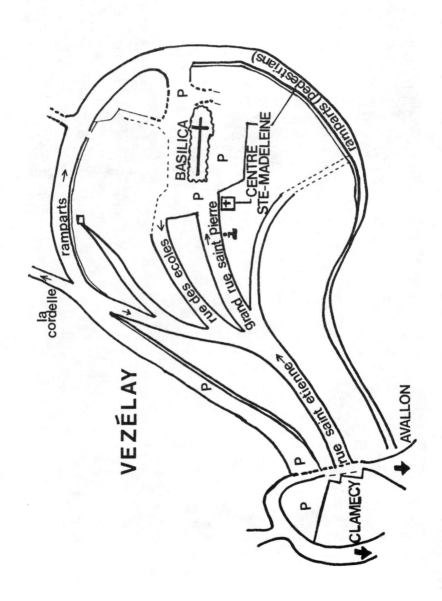

VEZÉLAY

VÉZELAY
REGION: BURGUNDY   DEPARTMENT: YONNE

WHAT TO SEE

Basilica of St. Mary Magdalene (Basilique Ste. Marie-Madeleine) At the top of Grande rue Saint Pierre (tel. 86-33-24-36). Open: Sunrise to sunset all year.

Considered a masterpiece of Romanesque architecture, the Basilica was built in the twelfth and thirteenth centuries. A piece of St. Mary Magdalene's relics, thought to be in Vézelay during the Middle Ages, is now lost or may be buried in a column shaft in the south transept. Guided tours in English are possible; inquire at the Presbytery to the right of the front of the Basilica. There are sound and light shows each night from June-October.

HOW TO GET THERE

By car: Autoroute A6 from Paris, exit Nitry-Vézelay; from Lyon exit Avallon. It is approximately 130 miles from Paris.

By public transport: Train, Station Sermizelles-Vézelay, 6 miles from Vézelay or Station Avallon, 10 miles from Vézelay. Taxi to Vézelay by Taxi les cars de la Madeleine (tel. 86-33-25-67).

WHERE TO STAY

Centre Sainte-Madeleine rue Saint Pierre, 89450 Vézelay (tel. 86-33-22-14).

Operated by the Franciscan Sisters of the Propagation of the Faith. 48 beds. No meals on site (café and restaurants in the Village). 40F for an individual room; 17-28F for dormitories.

TOURIST OFFICE

Syndicat d'Initiative, rue St. Pierre (tel. 86-33-23-69). Open: Apr.-Oct. Mon. and Tues.; Thurs.-Sat. 10am-1pm and 2-6pm; Sun. 10:30am-6:30pm; Nov.-Apr. closed.

NOTES

A major pilgrimage occurs on July 22, the Feast Day of St. Mary Magdalene. Spring through fall, there are musical concerts in the Basilica.

PARAY-LE-MONIAL

Visions of the Sacred Heart -
St. Margaret Mary Alacoque

*My divine Heart so passionately loves all men and you in par-
ticular that, no longer able to contain the flames of its burning
charity, it has to pour them forth through you...*
—First revelation of Jesus Christ to
St. Margaret Mary Alacoque, 1673

Like many mystics, initially, Margaret Mary Alacoque
was thought mad. For a time, some of her own sisters in
the Visitation Monastery in Paray-le-Monial would walk
by Margaret sprinkling holy water on her to ward off the
devil.

Margaret's ecstasies and visions, which began shortly
after she entered the convent at age twenty-four, almost
prevented her from taking her final vows as a nun; so
intense and enervating were her raptures that she couldn't
perform all of her convent duties. Threats of expulsion
hastened her prayers for help to Lord Jesus and she was
able to complete her vows.

Margaret almost had not entered the monastery at all.
As a teenager, she had spent four years bedridden with illness. She promised the Divine Mother she would become a
nun if she recovered her health. As soon as she has well,
however, she became interested in fine clothes and a social
life. After a while, Christ appeared to her and she returned
to her promise.

In Paray, the visions she had of Christ empowered her
with the mission of encouraging devotion to his Heart as
the sacred symbol of his love for humanity.

She was alone in her zeal until a well-respected and
brilliant young priest came to Paray and became her con-

fessor. Father Claude de la Colombière relieved Margaret's fears that she was delusional. He urged her to record her mystical experiences and eventually he lectured and wrote a book encouraging the devotion to the Sacred Heart. The book also authenticated an anonymous nun's revelations of the Sacred Heart. When her sisters at the convent read their esteemed confessor's book aloud one evening, they realized that his glowing references were to Margaret. Subsequently, her sisters changed and became some of Margaret's staunchest supporters in the rapid spread of the Sacred Heart devotion.

Though in good health at age forty-three, Margaret knew her death was near. To her superior she said, "*I now need only God alone...and to let myself be overwhelmed by the Heart of Christ.*"[21] She died in 1690 before there was even time to call a physician.

Were Christ a thousand times reborn in Bethlehem's stall and not in Thee, thou still art lost beyond recall.
—Angelus Silesius

Bascilica at Paray-le-Monial

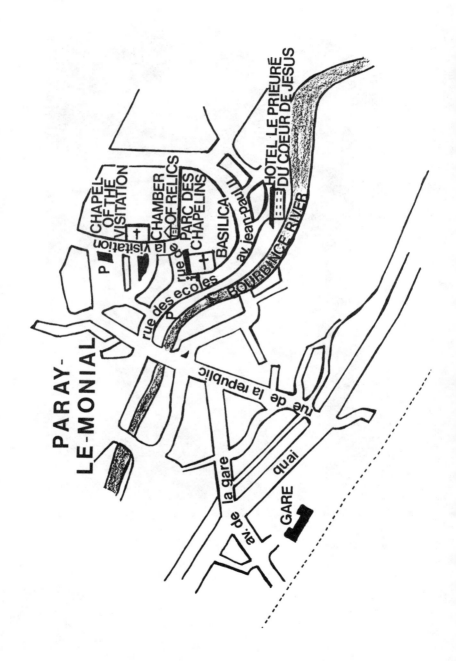

PARAY-LE-MONIAL
REGION: BURGUNDY
DEPARTMENT: SAÔNE-ET-LOIRE

WHAT TO SEE

Chapel of the Visitation (Sanctuary of the Apparitions), rue de la Visitation, 71600 Paray-le-Monial (tel. 85-81-09-95). Open: Daily, mornings and afternoons. Visitors are requested to refrain from visiting the chapel when a service is in progress.

It was in this Monastery chapel that St. Margaret received three revelations of Lord Jesus in 1673, 1674 and 1675. Her body is buried in the chapel. A guided tour of the chapel is possible; inquire in the adjacent gift shop.

Basilica of the Sacred Heart, (Place Alsace-Lorraine). Open: Mornings and afternoons, daily.

This twelfth century church built by the sixth abbot of Cluny is a miniature counterpart of the church at Cluny.

Parc des Chapelins is a large park behind the Basilica where major pilgrimage services are held. It contains a stations of the cross and in summer, a diorama of the life of St. Margaret.

Chamber of the Relics is a large room of articles which belonged to the saint including a reconstruction of the cell in which she lived. In an adjacent room, a slide presentation of the saint's life is shown at various times throughout the day for 8F. The Chamber is open mornings and afternoons from early April to late October. It is located behind the Basilica next to the park on rue de la Visitation.

HOW TO GET THERE

By car: Paray-le-Monial is on route N79-E62 between Mâcon and Moulins. Follow signs to Centre Ville to get to the sanctuaries and lodging. From Geneva (approximately

125 miles) take Autoroute A-40 or follow roads N206 to N84 to N75 to N79.

By public transport: Train, Station Paray-le-Monial. Lines Moulins/Lyon or Paris/Le Creusot. The station is within walking distance of lodging and sanctuaries (approximately 15 minutes).

WHERE TO STAY

Hotel le Prieuré du Coeur de Jesus, 8, av. Jean-Paul II, 71600 Paray-le-Monial (tel. 85-88-83-17).

The hotel is near the Basilica and other sanctuaries in a quiet, riverside setting. It is simply furnished, serving as a retreat house and religious conference center as well as a hotel. A chapel on the premises is available to guests. It has been recognized for its good cuisine. 10 rooms are available for handicapped. Elevator, parking. Approximately 107-167F per person per night for room with toilet and shower. Pension and demi-pension available.

TOURIST OFFICE

Office du Tourisme, located next to the Basilica. Open: Easter to the end of September; mornings and afternoons.

NOTES

On the Sunday nearest to October 16 there is a festival honoring the Feast Day of St. Margaret Mary Alacoque. Also, a major pilgrimage occurs in early June. In spring the lovely Burgundy countryside around Paray is full of color and frolicking calves and lambs.

XVIII
FRANCE

TAIZÉ

Contemporary Spiritual Community

Ah, Taizé, that little springtime!
—Pope John XXIII

Spring-like energy suddenly surrounds the pilgrim amidst placid farmlands and mustard fields of Burgundy. Blue tents, clusters of enthusiastic people and spontaneous song transform the landscape into a carnival-like mirage. The Taizé community is a dramatic contrast to many historical sacred sites of France; Taizé is sacredness in the making, a joyous celebratory holiness.

In 1940 twenty-five year old, Roger Louis Schutz-Marsauche, son of a Swiss Protestant minister, renounced a promising worldly future to form a unique religious community. He chose the tiny, poor hamlet of Taizé as the site for an ecumenical congregation of men striving to live by the highest Christian ideals of faith and service to others.

During the second world war, Brother Roger's community sheltered Jews and eventually was raided by the gestapo. After the war, it formed a cooperative to help the local farmers. Gradually, young people seeking deeper life meaning than materialism gravitated to the inspiring community.

Today, the community has grown and all year around individuals of all ages come for retreat, silence and worship.

The community also hosts special annual meetings of people ages seventeen to thirty from all over the world. To visit Taizé for a few hours or a few weeks is to receive an uplift of spiritual energy.

Ubi caritas et amor, Deus ibi est.
Where charity and love are, God is there.
                    —Words from *"Songs from Taizé,"* Ubi Caritas

Village of Taizé

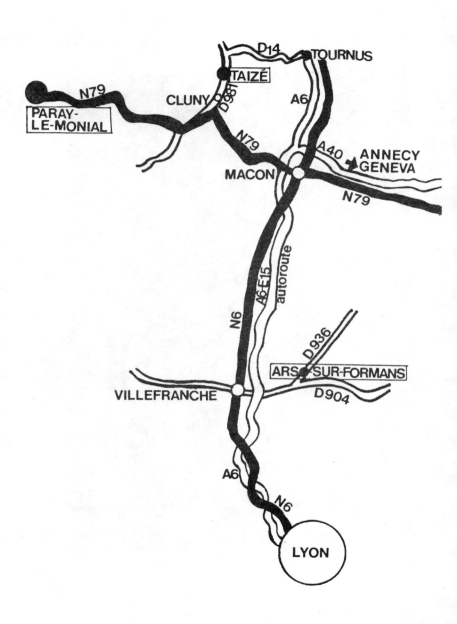

TAIZÉ
REGION: BURGUNDY
DEPARTMENT: SAÔNE-ET-LOIRE

WHAT TO SEE

The Church of Reconciliation This modern Church is the focus of Taizé services. Open: all hours.
The Village Church. Open: Dawn until dusk. An old, tiny Church in the nearby village is used by Taizé residents for individual meditation and prayer. The Community requests, however, that visitors do not wander through the tiny village but go directly to the Church.
The Exposition Store sells tapes, books and many items made by Taizé Brothers; the Community accepts no donations and supports itself through the sales in this store.

HOW TO GET THERE

By car: Autoroute A6, from the north, exit direction Tournus onto D14 and at Cormatin onto D981; from the south, on A6, exit at Mâcon-Sud onto N79, direction Moulins. Follow signs to Cluny on road D981 and after Cluny, follow signs to Taizé. Taizé is approximately 10 miles north of Cluny, 40 miles from Paray-le-Monial, 25 miles from Mâcon, and 85 miles from Geneva.
By public transport: Train, Station Chalon-sur-Saône or Mâcon-Ville or Mâcon-TGV (express train). Lines Paris via Lyon, Geneva or Chambery. There is a connecting bus service (about 25 miles) which runs on the line Chalon-Taizé-Cluny-Mâcon (SNCF timetable #576). Usually, a ticket can be purchased to cover both the train and bus transportation to Taizé.

WHERE TO STAY

Taizé Community, 71250 Cluny (tel. 85-50-14-14).

The Taizé Community welcomes pilgrims and retreatants who wish to become participants in the prayer, silence, study and worship at Taizé. Varied accommodations exist on a sliding scale fee basis from approximately 57-102F per person including meals. Handicapped in wheelchairs can be accommodated. Taizé is an easy daytrip from Paray-le-Monial by car (about 45 minutes). See the section on Paray for shelter there.

TOURIST OFFICE

No tourist office exists in Taizé, however, the Community has a welcome house which provides information.

NOTES

The Community regularly teaches beautiful songs in many languages to Taizé retreatants. The powerful music and words open the heart. Throughout the world, these songs are sung at Taizé services. At the Church of St.-Germaine des Prés in Paris every weekday about noon, a small group of people gather for simple worship and singing of the deeply moving chants of Taizé. All are welcome to attend.

ARS-SUR-FORMANS

The Mystic Curé d'Ars

I say nothing to Him;
I gaze at Him and He gazes at me.
How wonderful, my children, how wonderful!

—Curé d'Ars

In the early nineteenth century, Napoleon's police were looking for young Frenchmen avoiding the draft. The mystic Jean-Baptiste Vianney, age twenty, recently had been freed from labor on his peasant parents' land to attend school for the first time. He, like many Frenchmen of his day, did not believe in Napoleon's war. His schooling was interrupted for fourteen months while he hid from the police. Finally, he traded his inheritance with his brother who served his military assignment. Jean-Baptiste was able to complete his studies and be ordained a priest at age thirty. He was thought so unlearned by his superiors, however, that he was given the illiterate parish of Ars.

On the way to Ars, Jean-Baptiste stopped a young boy and asked directions. Prophetically, he told the boy that if he showed him the way to Ars, he would show the boy the way to heaven. Eventually, Jean-Baptiste, the Curé, led thousands Godward. A few years after he began his work in Ars word began to spread of his unusual gifts and powers. The isolated village quickly became a place of pilgrimage. Bishops, ministers of state, professional and business people from France and beyond were among the over twenty thousand people a year who sought the Curé's counsel during his forty years in Ars.

The Curé lived an ascetical life, eating and sleeping little. At 1am, he began hearing confessions; frequently, people waited five to twenty hours for their turn. The Curé often knew their pasts and futures before they spoke. His gifts also included miraculous healings and material-izations of physical sustenance needed for an orphanage he founded.

He said of the Virgin Mary, "'I loved her even before I knew her. My devotion to her is the oldest I possess.'"22 She appeared to him in his little house in Ars. The devil also appeared sometimes; witnesses were terrorized by the Curé's physical grapplings with demons while Jean-Baptiste was unperturbed.

Occasionally, the Curé tried to leave Ars permanently for solitude in a monastery; he never succeeded because his followers always induced him to return. In 1859, at age seventy-three, he died there. His body, incorrupt since his death, rests in the Ars Church. His life was an exemplary answer to the question he said God will ask each one of us,

*"He will ask if we used our strength to render service to our neighbor.'"*23

Bascilica at Ars

ARS-SUR-FORMANS
REGION: RHÔNE-ALPES DEPARTMENT: AIN

WHAT TO SEE

The Basilica of Ars, Open: Daily 8am-noon and 2-6pm. The Basilica was built after the Curé's death and within it are preserved chapels built by the Curé himself. Pope John Paul II was a pilgrim here in 1986. In the Basilica there is a reliquary containing the incorrupt body of the saint (only his face has been covered with wax) and a chapel to Our Lady of Ars which was the favorite of Jean-Baptiste.

The House of the Curé d'Ars is across a narrow street to the left of the Basilica. It is preserved as it was at the time of his death. He died in the bedroom upstairs.

The Chapel of the Curé's Heart near his home, is a chapel containing a reliquary with the Curé's heart. The heart was removed from his body when he was beatified in 1905.

HOW TO GET THERE

By car: Autoroute A6, exit Villefranche-sur-Saône (direction Bourg en Bresse). Ars is on route N904, 18 miles north of Lyon and approximately 95 miles from Geneva. It is not on a general map of France but on Michelin's Rhône-Alpes regional map #244.

By public transport: Train, Station Villefranche-sur-Saône (5½ miles from Ars). Lines Paris/Lyon or Paris/Mâcon. Bus or taxi to Ars from station.

WHERE TO STAY

La Providence 01480 Ars-sur-Formans (tel. 74-00-71-65). Operated by the Community of the Sisters of St. Joseph of Bourg. 33 rooms with 1 or 2 beds; 21 rooms with 2 beds and shower and toilet. Capacity to receive handicapped in wheelchairs. Elevator, dining room, meeting, chapel, parking. Pension or demi-pension available.

TOURIST OFFICE

A small tourist office is located to the left of the Basilica before reaching the Curé's house. Open: Mornings and afternoons, May through September.

NOTES

August is the Feast Day of St. Jean-Baptiste Vianney. Ars is a sweet, very tiny town of one main street. Don't miss the wonderful crêpes served at the crêperie across from the Basilica.

ANNECY

Divine Friendship -
Saint Francis de Sales and
Saint Jane Frances de Chantal

*You ask...What I desire should remain most deeply ingrained on
your mind. Ah! what shall I say to you, my most dear daughters,
but these two words? Desire nothing, refuse nothing.*
—St. Francis de Sales

St. Vincent de Paul, confessor to Jane Frances de
Chantal, was praying for her in Paris as she lay dying in
Moulins, France. Suddenly, he saw a shining ball of fire
rise from the earth and meet in the air another ball of fire;
both ascended to the heavens to merge into an immense
bright Light. A distinct interior voice told him the Light
represented the Divine Essence, and the two balls represented the souls of Jane Frances, who had just died, and
Francis de Sales, her spiritual guide, who had died nineteen years earlier.

Jane was born in 1572 and married at age twenty to a
wealthy Baron. Her married life was happy and busy with
the responsibilities of raising four children and running a
large household of servants. She spent her spare time in
the spiritual pursuits of prayer and reading religious
works. She prayed to be sent a spiritual guide. In response,
she had a vision of a man wearing a black cossack, white
vestment and headcap.

Jane's husband was killed in a hunting accident when
she was twenty-eight. Two years after her husband's death,
she saw the man of her vision preaching in a nearby town.
He was the visiting Bishop of Geneva, Francis de Sales.

Francis also recognized Jane from an earlier vision of his own.

Francis de Sales was born in 1567 near Annecy to an aristocratic family. He was a brilliant student who studied law and theology in Paris and Padua, Italy. His parents wanted him to obtain an important worldly position. A short time after he was admitted to the bar, however, he was thrown off his horse three times in succession, and each time his sword and scabbard landed on the ground in the form of a cross. Francis intuited this event to mean he should follow his heart's desire and become a priest. He did, and by the age of thirty-five, he was a Bishop.

After Jane and Francis met, a lifelong friendship and spiritual collaboration began. Eventually, Jane chose to dedicate her life solely to God. For many years, Francis had wanted to create a new religious order for women which would allow visitation of the sick and poor. In 1610, following this goal, Jane and two other women began the first monastery of the Visitation Order in Annecy.

For the next twelve years, Jane and Francis continued to found monasteries together all over France. Francis also counselled, lectured and wrote prolifically. His work, "Introduction to the Devout Life" is still a spiritual classic. In it he urged that "...it is a mistake...to exclude devoutness of life from among soldiers, from shops and offices...from the homes of the married ...Religious devotion does not destroy: it perfects."[24] Jane experienced many trials as the co-foundress and administrator of the over eighty Visitation Monasteries. She successfully overcame her difficulties by combining great administrative ability with a deep interior life.

In 1622 Francis suffered a stroke. Following the medical treatment of the day, he was bled and cauterized with an hot branding iron. He died soon after. Nineteen years later, his devoted friend Jane followed him in death and St. Vincent de Paul's vision of their ascendance together remains an inspiration for pilgrims to Annecy.

"*We must die,*"[inwardly, to the little self, the ego] said St. Francis de Sales, "*that God may live in us.*" For St. Jane de Chantal,"*the whole world would die of love for so amiable a God if I could make it feel the sweetness which a soul tastes in loving him.*"25

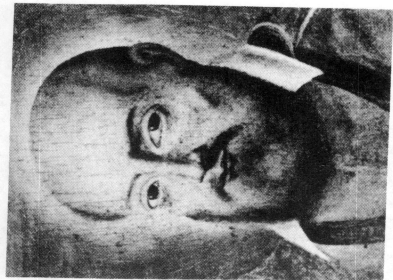

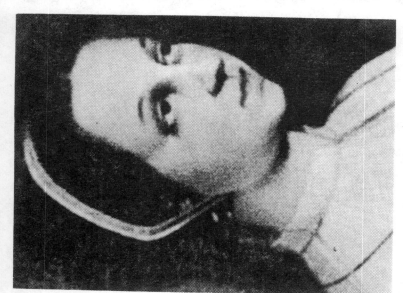

St. Jane Frances de Chantal and St. Francis de Sales

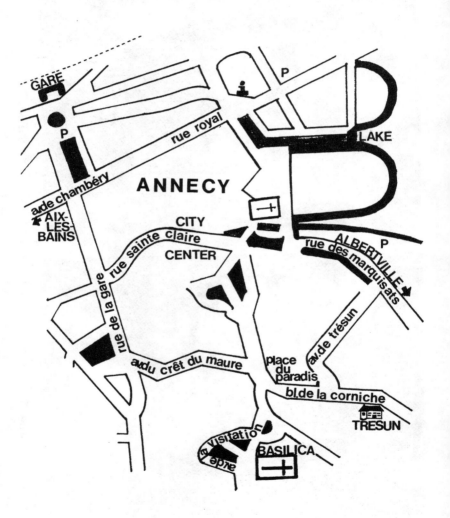

ANNECY
REGION: RHÔNE-ALPES
DEPARTMENT: HAUTE-SAVOIE

WHAT TO SEE

Basilica of the Visitation (La Basilique de la Visitation), 20, avenue de la Visitation, 74000 Annecy (tel. 50-45-22-76). Open: Mornings and afternoons, daily. A small museum and shop are next to the Basilica.

The sarcophagi containing the bodies of St. Francis de Sales and St. Jane de Chantal are in this sanctuary, which was built between 1922-1930. Both bodies had been hidden in a mattress and transported by a boat across Lake Annecy in 1793 by sisters of the Monastery of the Visitation in order to protect them from defilement during the French Revolution. After the Revolution, the bodies of the saints were kept in the Church of St. Francis in Annecy until the Basilica was constructed. St. Francis' body was found incorrupt when examined ten years after his death. St. Jane de Chantal's body was found incorrupt eighty-one years after her death. His heart, which was removed at death and placed in a reliquary in the Church of the Visitation in Lyon, has exuded a clear oil throughout the years. Her heart, which is kept in the Monastery of the Visitation in Nevers, periodically swells as if expressing grief.

The Church of St. Francis de Sales, 4 place Saint-Maurice, 74000 Annecy (tel. 50-45-06-92). Open: Mornings and afternoons.

This was the site of the first Visitation Order Monastery. The Church was consecrated in 1617 by St. Francis de Sales and restored in 1645. The place where the bodies of St. Francis and St. Jane rested until they were transferred to the Basilica is marked. A Black Madonna in the Church is similar to the one which was revered by St. Francis de Sales.

HOW TO GET THERE

By Car: Autoroute A40/41, exit Annecy-Sud, direction La Rive Ouest/Albertville to get to sights and shelter.
By public transport: Train, Station Annecy. Easily reached from Lyon, Grenoble, Chambery, Nice, etc. To get to sights or shelter, take a taxi or bus No. 1 (infrequent) and get off at stop "Paradis," place du Paradis, at the entrance to the Avenue of the Visitation; a short steep walk up this avenue leads to the Basilica.

WHERE TO STAY

Tresun, Centre Spirituel, 8 Boulevard de la Corniche, 74000 Annecy (tel. 50-45-33-21). A small, quiet retreat house operated by the Jesuit Fathers and the Sisters of St. Joseph of Annecy; it is located near Old Annecy and the sanctuaries. Approximately 100F, single room.

TOURIST OFFICE

Office du Tourisme, 1 rue Jean-Jaures, 74000 Annecy (tel.50-45-00-33). Open: 9am-noon and 2-5:30pm.

NOTES

December 12 is the Feast Day of St. Jane Frances de Chantal; January 24 is the Feast Day of St. Francis de Sales. Old Annecy, where the two saints worked and walked, is like a French Venice. Flower-lined canals flow through the city which is perched on the banks of reportedly the purest lake in Europe, Lake Annecy. Located near the Swiss border, Annecy is popular with tourists and can be an expensive place to visit. Yet, there are ample quiet nooks and sanctuaries wherein to seek the treasures spoken of by the saints.

XXI
FRANCE

LA SALETTE

Appearance of the Weeping Beautiful Lady

...If my people will not submit,
I shall be forced to let fall the arm of my Son...
I gave you warning last year...[the crops failed]
but you did not heed it.
> —The Beautiful Lady at La Salette

A weeping woman spoke these words to two young shepherds as they tended their cows in majestic and isolated foothills of the French Alps near Gap. Melanie Calvat, age fourteen, and Maximin Giraud, age eleven had eaten their cheese and bread on a beautiful day in September, 1846 and then napped on the grass. After awakening and finding their cows, Melanie saw a globe of fire near the fountain where they had slept. It was as if, in their words, "the sun had fallen there."26 The swirling light grew, expanded and opened, revealing a woman seated and weeping with her head in her hands. The children did not know who she was; they simply called her "The Beautiful Lady."

She was dressed like the peasant women of the region in a long dress and a covering apron. She was tall, wore a crown of roses and roses fringed the edges of her white shawl. Her brow radiated light; she seemed to be made of light.

She spoke with the children at length; expressing her sorrow about the state of mankind. Through the children she called to people to turn to spiritual living or else reap misery. She said there will come a great famine. Before the famine comes, "the children under seven years of age will be seized with trembling and will die in the hands of those who hold them; the others will do penance by the famine. The walnuts will become bad and the grapes will rot."27

The Divine Mother wept throughout her discourse with the children. She wished to spare the family of mankind further misery from wrong living so she urged the children to "make this [her message] well known to all my people."28 After many years of investigation, the Catholic Church authenticated the apparition of the Blessed Virgin at La Salette. Innumerable persons of many races and countries have since learned of and heeded her counsel by infusing their lives with the dynamism of daily prayer and meditation.

Today the sanctuary draws pilgrims year round. In the quiet seasons after summer and before Easter, it is not difficult to imagine a supernatural event occurring at the site.

*"The radiant vision now began to disappear. We saw her head no more, then the rest of her body no more; she seemed to melt away. There remained a great light...as well as the roses at her feet which I tried to catch with my hands; but there was nothing more. We looked for a long time...to see if we could have another glimpse of her.'"*29

The Weeping Beautiful Lady, La Salette

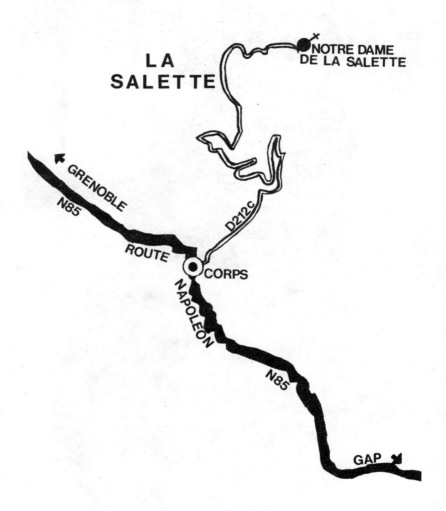

LA SALETTE
REGION: RHÔNE-ALPES DEPARTMENT: ISERE

WHAT TO SEE

Site of the Apparition, outdoors. Open: All hours, all year round, weather permitting.

The Sanctuary of La Salette is a retreatant's dream. If you desire beauty and quiet you can't beat this isolated site in the French Alps. It is only reachable by a narrow winding road which will take your breath away: 6000 foot mountains tower over lush farm valleys and waterfalls tumble by hamlets of houses and churches which seem unchanged from the time of the apparition. In the Sanctuary, rose colored clouds hug snow-capped mountain peaks at sunset and the night skies are full of stars. The silence is audible. In April or May you can enjoy the wildflowers emerging from crusts of snow one day and be snowed in the next day. A snow cover only adds to the majestic beauty of La Salette.

HOW TO GET THERE

By car: Route N85 from Grenoble (north, 45 miles) or from Gap (south, 33 miles) to Corps. The Sanctuary (not the same as the hamlet of La Salette-Fallavaux) is approximately 10 miles, 25 minutes, from Corps up a windy, picturesque road. In winter, the route is kept open from snow; however, in case of bad weather, it's advisable to call the Hôtellerie at the Sanctuary in advance to check road conditions. Geneva is approximately 105 miles from the sanctuary. The sanctuary is not on a general map of France; use Michelins Rhône-Alpres Regional map #244.
By public transport: Train, Station Gap (33 miles) or Grenoble (45 miles). During July and August, there are daily transport services direct from Grenoble to the Sanctuary. Taxi services are available at other times for

approximately 100F from Gap which is the better off-season arrival choice. For taxi from Gap call: Gap-Cars Alpes Littoral S.C.A.L. (tel. 92-51-06-05). For taxi from Grenoble call: Gare Routière de Grenoble (tel. 76-47-77-77).

WHERE TO STAY

L'Hôtellerie du Sanctuaire Notre Dame de la Salette, 38970 La Salette-Fallavaux (tel. 76-30-00-11).

It is an effort to reach La Salette by car or public transportation because of its remote location so plan on staying overnight there. The only place to stay at the Sanctuary is a large Hôtellerie. The Hôtellerie adjoins a Basilica, cafe, pilgrim's shop, dining hall and other amenities in an enclosed mall. Ask for a room with a view of the mountains. If you desire company on your pilgrimage you can easily meet people in the dining hall which will be busy with pilgrims around Easter, Christmas and during the summer.

Operated by the Association of Pilgrims of La Salette. 450 beds, 250 rooms, some with WC and shower. Closed November. Lengths of stay limited to 3 days in summer. Demi-pension and pension. Rates from 58-94F single; 39-75F doubles per person (rates are tiered and drop after 2, 3 and 4 or more nights).

TOURIST OFFICE

None exists at the Sanctuary; the pilgrim's shop, however, has information on La Salette.

NOTES

September 19, the anniversary of the apparition, is celebrated at the Sanctuary with a pilgrimage procession. There is also a procession on Good Friday and on August 15. Panoramic hikes and picnics in the fresh alpine air are a must at La Salette.

LA SAINTE-BAUME

Cave of St. Mary Magdalene

...Woman why weepest thou? Whom seekest thou? She, suppos-
ing him to be the gardener, saith unto him, Sir, if thou have
borne him hence, tell me where thou hast laid him, and I will take
him away. Jesus saith unto her, Mary. She turned herself, and
saith unto him, Rabboni; which is to say, Master.

—John 20: 15-16

What happened to Christ's women disciples after his resurrection? One tradition says they were set adrift from Palestine in an oarless boat without sails. The miraculous voyagers landed on a beach in southern France now called the Saint Marys of the Sea, Les Saintes Maries-de-la-Mer.

Mary Jacob, Mary Salome and a black servant named Sara stayed in Stes. Maries; Martha, Lazarus' sister went to nearby Tarascon; Mary Magdalene, sister of Martha, went alone inland to a mountain range called La Sainte-Baume, the holy cave.

Mary Magdalene was the first of Lord Jesus' followers to see and proclaim his resurrection. Earlier in her life, Mary Magdalene had been a beautiful and wealthy courtesan to the Romans who ruled Palestine. She had great freedom, owned property and socialized with friends in the Roman court. She gave this all up to follow her Master.

Some of Jesus' disciples urged him not to associate with a woman of Mary Magdalene's past. Jesus not only forgave her, he prophesized that the world would remember and honor her life. This independent, strong woman was revered during the Middle Ages by a large following of devotees including saints like St. Francis of Assisi. "According to certain traditions it was through the Magdalene rather than through Peter and the male apostles, that Jesus transmitted his secret doctrine."[30] Over the centuries, as patriarchy increased, "...all the writings that extolled the role of Mary were ultimately excluded from the canon."[31]

According to the Provence legend of her life, after Jesus' resurrection, she reached southern France by a miraculous voyage. Then she went to an extraordinary site where pagans had worshipped. Here, she lived the last thirty-three years of her life preaching and meditating in a large cave. Symbolic of her inner exaltation is the tradition that seven times daily she was lifted to a mountain by angels to hear the music of heaven.

When Mary sensed death's approach she walked to the village of Villa Latta where Maximin, also a disciple of Christ, received her, and buried her upon her death. Eventually, Cassian monks were entrusted with her remains. In 710, Saracens invaded the area. The monks removed several pieces of bone from Mary's body and sent them to Rome and Vézelay for safekeeping. They hid the rest of the body, and knowledge of its location became lost.

Centuries later, a nephew of King Louis of France searched for the body; in 1279, he found a sarcophagus in the town of St. Maximin, formerly Villa Latta. When it was opened, a sweet perfume odor permeated the area for several days. In the tomb was a ball of wax concealing a parchment. The paper declared that the remains were those of Mary Magdalene. When the bone of the saint which had been preserved in Rome fit perfectly into the lower jaw of the discovered skeleton, Pope Boniface VIII declared the remains to be those of Mary Magdalene.

Pilgrimage to her cave, the La Sainte-Baume, is a unique experience. The only access is a path through a virgin forest of limes, beeches and maples. The rare woods, not found anywhere else south of the latitudes of Paris, are now a government preserve. Approximately an hour's walk steadily uphill on a route once traversed by St. Catherine of Siena, St. Vincent de Paul, St. Jane de Chantal and other saints, leads to the unusual cave at a 3,105 foot altitude in the Sainte-Baume Massif. The hike is rewarded by extraordinary views of the surrounding countryside.

Other pilgrimage sites associated with the women disciples of Christ exist in France. In nearby Tarascon every year on July 29, St. Martha'a Feast Day, there is a religious celebration at the church where St. Martha's bones are kept.

The bones of Mary Salome and Mary Jacob and Sarah were found in Stes. Maries de-la-Mer in 1448, and are still buried in the town's Romanesque church. Mary Salome became the patron saint of Provence. Sara, her black servant, became the patron saint of the gypsies. Each year on May 24 and 25, gypsies from all around the world gather at Stes. Maries-de-la-Mer to elect their new queen and to make a celebratory procession to the sea.

...why trouble ye the woman? for she hath wrought a good work upon me...Verily I say unto you, wheresoever this gospel shall be preached in the whole world, there shall also this, that this woman hath done, be told for a memorial of her.

—Matthew 26: 10,13

St. Mary Magdalene

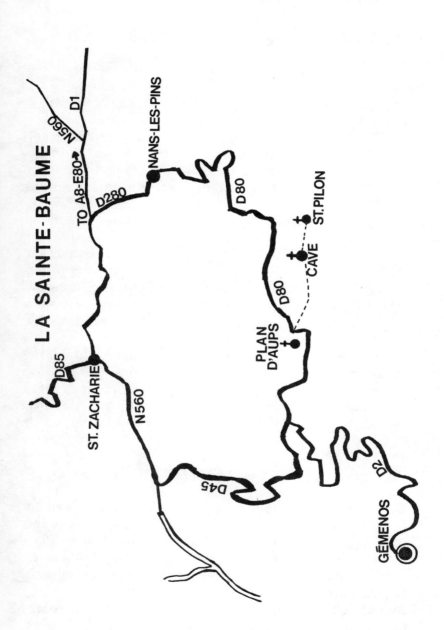

LA SAINTE-BAUME
REGION: PROVENCE   DEPARTMENT: VAR

WHAT TO SEE

The Cave of Saint Mary Magdelene. Open: Mornings through afternoons, all year around.

The large cave has been converted to an unusual church of several chapels and six altars. Behind the high altar is a relic (femur) of the Saint. The cave drips water thought to have healing powers. There is a small pilgrim's store next to the cave.

St. Pilon is a small chapel fifty feet above the cave (approximately thirty-five minutes from the cave). It marks the summit where St. Mary was purportedly lifted daily by angels. It is a $1^1/_2$ hour walk from a point called the oratory crossroads; it is approximately a 2 hour walk from the base where the path to the cave begins. Both sites have extraordinary panoramas. Open: Mornings through afternoons, all year around.

The Basilica of St. Mary Magdalene (Basilique de St. Marie Madeleine). Open: mornings and afternoons.

In the town of St. Maximin, 11 miles from the cave, is the Church where St. Mary Magdalene's remains are buried in the crypt. Open: Mornings and afternoons, daily.

HOW TO GET THERE

By car: Autoroute A8-E80-La Provincale. Exit St. Maximin La Sainte-Baume. Follow the signs toward Nans-les-Pins on D280. At Nans-les-Pins continue on toward Plan d'Aups on D80 where you will see the Hôtellerie (approximately 11 miles from St. Maximin-La Sainte-Baume exit).

By public transport: La Sainte-Baume is not easy to reach by public transport. Train, Station Marseille St. Charles (approximately 21 miles) or Toulon (approximately 30 miles). It is then necessary to go by bus/van (tel. 91-08-16-40) via the route for Cuges, Gémanos, St. Zacharie, Nan-les-Pins, Rougiers, St. Maximin, Plan d'Aups, La Sainte-Baume. From Toulon, white autocars (opposite the train station) via route Signes, Méounes, LaRoquebrussane (tel. 94-92-97-41).

WHERE TO STAY

La Sainte-Baume is within a 2-3 hours drive of Nice and the French Riviera, as well as Marseilles, Aix-en-Provence and Arles so that it is possible to visit it as a daytrip. There is a spartan pilgrim's hostel, the Hôtellerie La Sainte-Baume at the sanctuary. It was built in the mid-nineteenth century style, on the plateau at the base of the ascent to the cave.

Hôtellerie de La Sainte-Baume (tel. 42-04-54-84), operated by the Dominican community. Singles approximately 70F. Demi-pension available, with an affordable restaurant next door.

If you wish to stay in Nice, try the following:

La Maison du Seminaire, 29 Boulevard Franck Pilatte, 06300 Nice (tel. 93-89-39-57).

Operated by the Diocese of Nice. 32 modern rooms, 70 beds, some with private bath, all with sink. Parking, elevator, library, chapel. About a mile from central Nice. Located next to the sea and gardens, ask for a room with a view of the sea; it's extraordinary! Reserve as early as possible by mail or phone. 130F single room without bath. Complete pension 215-285F per person; demi-pension also available. To reach La Maison by car take Autoroute A101 exit Nice-Est. Follow the direction of the Port (blue sign with boat symbol). At the Port, turn left and follow the road alongside the sea. After approximately 500 meters, the Maison du Séminaire is on the left. If traveling by public transport, ask for directions when you call the Retreat House.

TOURIST OFFICE

Syndicat D'Initiative de St. Maximin-La Sainte-Baume, Place de l'Hôtel de Ville (next to the Basilica) (tel. 94-78-00-09). Open: Mornings and evenings, April through October.

NOTES

On St. Mary Magdalene's Feast Day, July 22, a midnight mass is celebrated in the cave. Occasionally, musical concerts by artists such as the pan flutist Zamfir, are held in the cave. Inquire in the small pilgrim's shop next to the cave.

If you stay in Nice and like the multi-colored onion domes of Russian Orthodox Churches, see the exotic Russian Orthodox Cathedral in Nice. Open: mornings and afternoons except for Sunday morning and Orthodox Feast Days (tel. 93-96-88-02). Also, Nice is famous for its art museums and its Carnival held at the end of February.

XXIII
FRANCE

ROCAMADOUR

Celestial Center on the Journey to the Star

> *Je suis noire, et je suis belle*
> *I am black and I am beautiful*
> —Song of Solomon 1:5

In exhilarating, secluded country, a chateau, a walled religious city and a village seem to cascade ethereally down a high cliff overlooking a vast panoramic gorge.

According to legend, in 1166 Benedictine monks found an incorrupt body in a cliffside cave at the area now called Rocamadour. The body was thought to be that of a hermit named Amadour. One tradition believes that Amadour was Zacchaeus mentioned in the Bible who came to France to preach the gospel. The site he chose had been inhabited since prehistoric times and was a center of Druid worship. As a result of the discovery of Amadour's incorrupt body, Rocamadour became a popular stopping place on the famous pilgrimage to Santiago de Compostela "The Field of the Star," in Spain.

The Madonna revered at the sanctuary since the Middle Ages is black. There are many Black Virgin images reigning on the altars of churches in southern France. Many believe they originated with the Egyptian pre-Christian goddess Isis who was dark colored. Others believe the Black Madonnas in France were modeled after the female image in the Song of Solomon. The song's reference to blackness and beauty, however, is thought to refer to an interior darkness, the charcoal-like ego, covering the divine beauty of the image of God within. Still others insist that the Black Virgins, which are highly popular throughout the world, are no symbol at all, only the result of the smoke from candles darkening white madonnas!

During the Middle Ages, Saints Dominic and Bernard, King Louis, Queen Eleanor of Aquitaine and other luminaries of their day all carried images of the powerful feminine in their hearts. They revered the Black Virgin of Rocamadour and traversed the 216 stone steps to her shrine on their knees.

Today, Rocamadour's sanctuary, wooded paths and preserved medieval village make it one of the major tourist centers in southeast France. Its single street is overcrowded in summer, yet its population dwindles to about forty in winter. It is best to visit the spectacular, remote site in early spring or early fall. Be sure to view the town from the nearby hamlet of L'Hospitalet. Here, ruins of a medieval hospice, pilgrim's lodging, mark the place where medieval pilgrims paused for view of the sanctuary. Exalting in its incredible sight they named the viewpoint "Montjoie" mount of joy. With difficulty, they turned away from the glorious vista to continue their journey to the "field of the star," Santiago de Compostela.

He who binds to himself a joy does the winged life destroy; But he who kisses the joy as it flies lives in eternity's sun rise.
—William Blake

Rocamadour

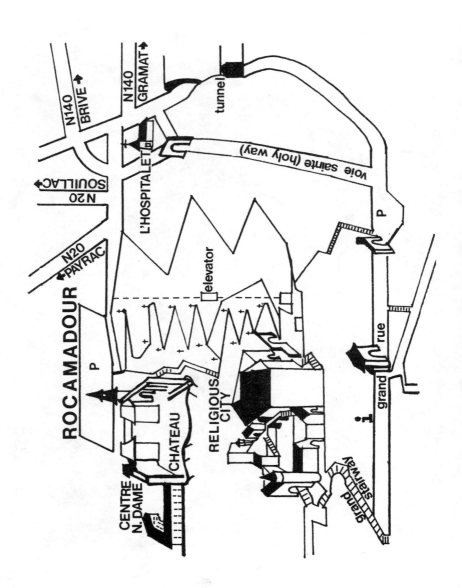

ROCAMADOUR

REGION: MIDI-PYRÉNEES　　DEPARTMENT: LOT

WHAT TO SEE

The Seven Chapels of the Religious City
The Miraculous Chapel - Our Lady of Rocamadour (Notre-Dame Chapelle), in the Religious City (tel. 65-33-63-29). Open: Mornings and afternoons.

A statue of the Black Virgin of Rocamadour, prototype of the numerous Black Madonnas of southern France, sits on an altar built over a Druid stone. Among her attributes are miraculous powers: She frees captives, promotes fertility, protects sailors, and resuscitates unbaptised babies. Above the portico of the Chapel is a sword thrust deep into the rock. According to tradition, it is Roland's cutlass, the Durandal, which he dedicated to the Lady before joining Charlemagne to fight the Saracens in Spain.

Also in the Religious City are the *Chapels of St. John the Baptist, St. Blase, St. Michael, St. Amadour* ("the Crypt"), *St. Anne* and the *St. Savior Basilica.* Only the Basilica and the Chapel of Our Lady of Rocamadour are open all year round. St. Amadour's and St. Michael's may be visited as part of a guided tour (June - mid-September, daily except Sun., from 9am-6pm) or by individual appointment. Inquire at the pilgrim's shop located in the forecourt of the Religious City. A small museum is also in the forecourt, admission 10F.

The Grand Escalier or *Stairway* which was travelled by pilgrims on their knees connects the village to the Religious City.

The Way of the Cross is a beautiful, wooded path, gradually sloped, linking the Religious City to the Chateau above it. There is also an elevator which connects the two for 9F.

The Chateau was built above the Holy City to protect it. A religious community now dwells in the Chateau and it is not open to the public. However, its ramparts offer spectacular views and can be toured for 6F.

HOW TO GET THERE

By car: Rocamadour is approximately 34 miles from Brive and 39 miles from Cahors on route N20-E09. Take road D673 off of route N20 (or off of N140 if coming from Figeac). Follow signs to Rocamadour.
By public transport: Train, Station Rocamadour-Padirac (2 1/2 miles from Rocamadour). Lines Paris/Brive Rodez and Brive/Capderiac/Toulouse. Taxi (tel. 65-33-70-50) and Autocar (tel. 65-33-62-12) to Rocamadour.

WHERE TO STAY

Le Centre d'Accueil Notre-Dame (Le Chateau), 46500 Rocamadour (tel. 65-33-63-29). Operated by the religious community living in the Chateau. Open all year except December. 60 beds; 46 rooms; 9 for couples; sink in each; 18 with toilet. Parking, chapel, dining room, conference rooms. Demi-pension or pension around 160F for one person. To get to the Retreat House, at the hamlet of L'Hospitalet, take the direction to "Le Chateau." Ask for a room with a view of the rocky gorge.

TOURIST OFFICE

Syndicat d'Initiative, Hôtel de Ville (tel. 65-33-62-59). Open: Apr.-Sept. 10am-noon and 3-7pm; July and Aug. 10am-noon and 3-8pm. Will change currency as there is no bank in Rocamadour. In summer, there is a branch office of the Syndicat at L'Hospitalet (tel. 65-33-62-80).

NOTES

There are annual pilgrimages during the week of September 8. (September 8 is the day celebrated as the Nativity of the Virgin Mary). Also, there is a torchlight procession from L'Hospitalet to the sanctuary on the evening of August 14 (the night before Assumption Day) and celebrations on May 1, St. Amadour's Feast Day.

LE PUY

The Black Madonna

Hail, Holy Queen, Mother of mercy; hail, our life, our sweetness and our hope. To you do we cry...
— A portion of the Salve Regina, Anthem of Le Puy

"Death," demanded the crowds, as the blindfolded feminine form was pushed towards the executioner's block. The guillotine dropped, severing her head but no blood flowed because it was the statue of the Black Madonna that was being destroyed by the French Revolutionists of 1794. The Revolutionists believed the Church was part of the established order oppressing their lives; they sought to eradicate every symbol of the Church's power.

According to legend, the Madonna's cult began at Le Puy in 46 A.D. when she appeared on Mount Anis, a site of Druid worship. She again appeared on the Mount in 430 near a black dolmen, a sacred stone. The apparition told a widow who suffered from malignant fevers to lie on the stone; she was miraculously healed. Later, the fantastic tradition continued when a local bishop, at the site during a freak July snowstorm, saw a stag run out of the woods and trace the design of a cathedral in the snow. The bishop built a basilica on the site; later, it became the cathedral dedicated to the Black Virgin of Le Puy.

The unique geography of Le Puy no doubt contributed to its ancient recognition as a place of mystery. Four startling volcanic precipices encircle the city. The Cathedral to Our Lady of Le Puy is built on one outcrop; a tenth century chapel to St. Michael on another; an enormous Mother and Child on the third; and a statue of St. Joseph and the Infant Jesus rest on the fourth.

Le Puy's greatest glory was during the Middle Ages when it was one of the four main starting points for thousands of travelers who pilgrimaged to Santiago de Compostela in Spain. Charlemagne, St. Antony of Padua, St. Dominic and numerous Popes, Kings and Queens came to worship the Black Madonna at Le Puy. St. Joan of Arc sent her mother and brothers to Le Puy to pray to the Lady for her victory at Orléans.

Though it can be dark and dreary on sunless days, Le Puy still charms pilgrims who can be seen with backpacks starting on the route to Spain perhaps singing, as did the Crusaders marching to the Holy Land, the Salve Regina.

..to you do we send up our sighs, mourning and weeping in this valley of tears. Turn, then, most gracious Advocate, your eyes of mercy toward us...

The Black Madonna, Our Lady of Le Puy

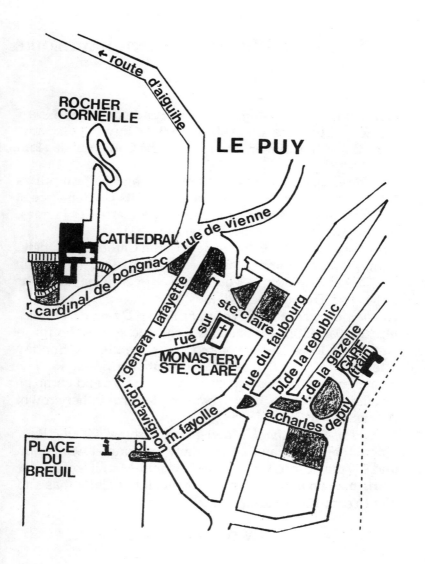

LE PUY-EN-VELAY

REGION: AUVERGNE DEPARTMENT: HAUT-LOIRE

WHAT TO SEE

Cathedral of Our Lady of Le Puy (Cathédrale de Notre Dame du Puy), rue des Tables, 43000, Le Puy. Open: 8am-6pm, daily. In summer, free tours of the Cathedral at 11am and 3:30pm.

The Cathedral is built half on rock and half on pillars into the hillside of Mt. Anis. In front of its Golden Gate at the main entrance is the fever stone, La Pierre des Fièvres, which purportedly healed the widow.

Cloister of the Cathedral is next to the Cathedral. Open: 9am-noon and 2-6pm, daily except Thursday. Admission 16F; ticket also admits you to the adjacent Chapel of the Relics and Treasury of Religious Art.

Rocher Corneille and Statue of Notre Dame de France. Open: 10am-5pm most of the year and longer hours in summer. Closed December and January except on Sunday afternoon; closed Tuesdays, November 1-March 15. The hearty can walk the steep climb to the statue and climb an interior stairway to an observation platform in her crown. Admission 8F.

Chapel of St. Michael, Montee Goutheron, 43000, Le Puy. Open: 10am-noon and 2-6pm, daily; in summer, 9am-noon and 2-7pm. Closed November to mid-March except for Christmas holidays when it is open all but Christmas and New Year's Days. Admission 7F.

HOW TO GET THERE

By car: Route A47 and N88 from Lyon (80 miles, approximately 2 hours); or, route N9/N102 from Clermont-Ferrand (approximately 80 miles, 2 hours).

By public transport: Train, Station Le Puy. Trains run to Le Puy from St. Étienne and Lyon directly; from Clermont-Ferrand or Nîmes, change trains at tiny St. George d'Aurac. Within Le Puy, for those not walking up to the sights, there are taxis (tel. 71-0542-43) and in summer, there is a small tourist train (Petit Train Touristique) which conducts a 45 minute tour through the city every hour between 9am-noon and 2-7pm for 24F.

WHERE TO STAY

Monastery of Saint Clare, 2, rue Saint Claire, 43000 Le Puy (tel. 71-09-17-47). 11 rooms, 20 person maximum. If full, try the *Hotel Bristol* 7, Avenue Maréchal-Foch (tel. 71-09-13-38) within walking distance of the train station. Parking, elevator, restaurant, 160-230F.

TOURIST OFFICE

Office de Tourisme, Place du Breuil, 43000 le Puy-en-Velay (tel. 71-09-38-41). Open: Mon.-Sat. 8:30am-noon and 2-6:30pm; in summer, Mon.-Sun. 8am-7pm.

NOTES

At Our Lady of Le Puy Cathedral there are celebrations on March 25 (Annunciation Day), July 1 (Visitation Day), August 15 (Assumption Day); and September 8 (the Nativity of the Blessed Virgin Mary). Also, there is a pilgrimage called the Procession of the Penitents on the Thursday before Easter.

ENDNOTES

1Nesta de Robeck, The Life of St. Francis of Assisi (Assisi: Casa Editrice Francescana Frati Minori Conventuali, 1975), 24.

2Piero Bargellini, The Little Flowers of Saint Clare, trans. Fr. Edmund O'Gorman (Padua: Messaggero Editions, 1988), 30.

3Marion A. Habig, Editor, St. Francis of Assisi Writings and Early Biographies (Chicago: Francisan Herald Press, 1972), 318.

4 P. Stefano, Sala, O.S.A., St. Clare of the Cross Montefalco Augustinian (Terni: Livoni, 1976), 5.

5Ibid. p. 10.

6Ibid. p. 14.

7C. Bernard Ruffin, Padre Pio: The True Story (Huntington, Indiana: Our Sunday Visitor, Inc., 1982), 301.

8Pope St. Gregory The Great, Life and Miracles of St. Benedict (Collegeville, Minnesota. The Liturgical Press, 1949), 67.

9Ibid. p. 70.

10Ibid p. 71.

11Fr. Joseph Santarelli, Loreto The Shrine of the Holy House Spiritual Guide, trans. S. Dougal (Loreto: Universal Congregation of the Holy House, 1989), 14.

12 Joseph I. Dirvin, C. M., Saint Catherine Labouré of the Miraculous Medal (Illinois: Tan Books and Publishers, Inc., 1984), pp. 83-84.

13Ibid. p. 100.

14Ibid. p. 93.

15Ibid. p. 94

16Ibid., p. 111

17Ibid. p. 187

18Blanche Merz, Point of Cosmic Energy, trans. M. C. Burdet (Essex, England: The C. W. Daniel Company, limited, 1987).

19Frances Parkinson Keyes, Bernadette of Lourdes (Hampshire England: Chapel River Press, 1975), p. 58.
20Ibid. p. 86.
21Jean Ladame, Saint Margaret Mary and the Visitation in Paray, trans. E. T. Dubois (Lescuyer-Lyon), 19.
22The Curé of Ars, A Pilgrim's Guide (Lescuyer - Lyon), 11.
23The Curé of Ars, Devotion Card (Le Puy: Ed. Y. Mappus).
24Alban Butler, The Lives of the Fathers, Martyrs, and other Principal Saints (London: Virtue and Company Limited, 1936).
25Ibid. pp. 973-974.
26The Association of Pilgrims of La Salette, La Salette The Apparition and The Message, p.8.
27Ibid. p. 11.
28Ibid. p. 13
29Ibid. p. 14
30Ean Begg. The Cult of the Black Virgin (London: Arkana, 1986), pp. 128-129.
31Ibid.

SELECT BIBLIOGRAPHY

Attwater, D. The Penguin Dictionary of Saints. 2d ed., rev. C.R. John. London: Penguin Books, 1983.

Balado, J.L. The Story of Taizé. 3d ed. London: A.R. Mowbray & Co. Ltd., 1988.

Ball, A. Modern Saints Their Lives and Faces. Rockford, IL: Tan Books and Publishers, Inc. 1983.

Bargellini, P. The Little Flowers of St. Clare. Trans. Fr. E. O'Gorman. Assisi: Edizioni Porziuncola, n.d.

Begg, E. The Cult of the Black Virgin. London: Arkana, 1985.

Bourdarias, J., M. Wasielewski. Guide des Chemins de Compostelle. Rennes: Fayard, 1989.

Butler, A. The Lives of the Fathers, Martyrs and Other Principal Saints. London: Virtue and Company, Limited, 1936.

Cambiaso, G.N. Le Colline della Speranza. Assisi: Citta della Editrice, 1987.

Carretto, C. I, francis. Trans. R.R. Barr. Maryknoll, NY: Orbis Books, 1982.

Carroll, L. The Annotated Alice - Alice's Adventures in Wonderland and Through the Looking Glass. Intro. and Notes by M. Gardner. New York: New American Library, 1974.

Craig, M. Spark from Heaven The Mystery of the Madonna of Medjugorje. Notre Dame, IL: Ave Maria Press, 1988.

Cruz, J.C. The Incorruptibles. Rockford, IL: Tan Books and Publishers, Inc., 1977.

Relics. Huntington, IN: Our Sunday Visitor, Inc., 1984.

Curé of Ars: A Pilgrim's Guide. Lescuyer-Lyon, n.d.

Delaney, J.J. ed. A Woman Clothed with the Sun: Eight Great Appearances of Our Lady. New York: Image Books, 1961.

DeRobeck, N. The Life of St. Francis of Assisi. Assisi: Casa Editrice Francescana Frati Minori Conventuali, 1975.

Desbonnets, P.T. Assisi in the Footsteps of St. Francis, Spiritual Guidebook. Trans. Sr. N. Celaschi, 1971.

Dirvin, Fr. J.I. St. Catherine Labouré of the Miraculous Medal. 1958. Reprint. Rockford, IL: Tan Books and Publishers, Inc., 1984.

Devoucoux du Buysson, Fr. P. Histoire abrégée de la Sainte-Baume. La Sainte-Baume: la Fraternité Sainte-Marie-Madeleine, 1989.

Faricy, R., L. Pecoraio. Mary Among Us The Apparitions at Oliveto Citra. Steubenville, OH: Franciscan University Press, 1989.

Fulop-Miller, R. Saints that Moved the World. 1945. Reprint. Salem, NH: Ayer Company, Publishers, Inc., 1987.

Habig, M.A. ed. St. Francis of Assisi, Omnibus of Sources. Chicago: Franciscan Herald Press, 1973.

Jacobs, M. A Guide to Provence. London: Penguin Group, 1989.

Keyes, F.P. Bernadette of Lourdes. 3d ed. Wheathampstead, Hertfordshire: Anthony Clarke, 1975.

Klauder, F.J., ed. Every Day with St. Francis de Sales. 2d ed. New Rochelle, NY: Don Bosco Multimedia, 1988.

LaDame, J. Saint Margaret Mary and the Visitation in Paray. Trans. E.T. Dubois. Heliogravure Lescuyer-Lyon, 1977.

La Salette: The Apparition and the Message. The Association of Pilgrims of La Salette, n.d.

Marnham, P. Lourdes A Modern Pilgrimage. New York: Coward, McCann, and Geoghegan, Inc., 1981.

Mauriac, F. Saint Margaret of Cortona. Trans. B. Frechtman. New York: Philosophical Library, 1948.

Merz, B. Points of Cosmic Energy. Trans. M.C. Burdet. Saffron Walden, Essex: C.W. Daniel Company Limited, 1987. Michelin Green Guides: Burgundy, France, French Riveria, Italy, Provence.

Nolan, M.L. and S. Christian Pilgrimage in Modern Western Europe Raleigh: University of North Carolina Press, 1989.

Pastrovicchi, Fr. A. St. Joseph of Copertino. Trans. Rev. F.S. Laing. 1918. Reprint. Rockford, IL: Tan Books and Publishers, Inc., 1980.

Pope St. Gregory the Great. Life and Miracles of St. Benedict. Collegeville, MN: The Liturgical Press, 1949.

Ruffin, C.B. Padre Pio: The True Story. Huntington, IN: Our Sunday Visitor, Inc., 1982.

Scofield, C.I., ed. The Scofield Reference Bible. New York: Oxford University Press, 1945.

Scudder, Vida D. Trans. and ed. Saint Catherine as seen in Her Letters. New York: E.P. Dutton & Co., 1906.

Sing, S.S. A Pilgrim in Assisi: Searching for Francis Today. Cincinnati: St. Anthony Messenger Press, 1981.

Songs from Taizé. Musique J. Berthier. Cluny: Ateliers et Presses de Taize, n.d.

Taylor, J.W. The Coming of the Saints. 1969. Reprint. Thousand Oaks, CA: Artisan Sales, 1985.

INDEX

SACRED FOOTSTEPS

A TRAVELER'S GUIDE
TO SPIRITUAL PLACES OF ITALY & FRANCE

ORDER FORM

If you would like to purchase copies of Sacred Footsteps, or would like information on a tour to Sacred Places in Italy and France when available, please fill out the following order form.

Please send me:

___ Copies of Sacred Footsteps at $9.95 each plus $3.55 shipping and handling, for a total of $13.50 each.

I am enclosing a check for $_____
I understand that I may return any book within 30 days for a full refund if I am not satisfied.

Your name and   _____
address

                    _____

                    _____

send to: **Opal Star Press**
(and make check   **P.O. Box 231512**
payable to:)   **Encinitas, CA 92023-1512**

10% of all proceeds are donated to charitable organizations.